". . . *a rare book whic*___ _____ _____ ___ ___ *al, emo-tional, and spiritual dynamics of depression . . . it will educate those who believe depression is merely a lack of faith.*"

Dr. Sidney Draayer, Director
Christian Counseling Center
Grand Rapids, Michigan

". . . *this story exhibits how the Christian community can understand and assist in the healing process of a disease which for too long has not been dealt with in an open and compassion-ate way.*"

Rodney Mulder, Ph.D., M.S.W.
Professor of Social Work
Grand Valley State College

". . . *intensely personal yet carefully researched.*"

Rev. Gerald R. Erffmeyer
Alger Park Christian Reformed Church

". . . *both candid and honest with regard to the patience and long-suffering needed in the overall healing of a significant depression.*"

D. Stephen King, M.D.
Staff Psychiatrist
Pine Rest Christian Hospital

". . . *the openness and sensitivity of this scholarly work make it a unique contribution to the literature on depression.*"

Catherine Hole, Ph.D.
Clinical Psychology

A SEASON
of
SUFFERING

A SEASON
of
SUFFERING

*One Family's
Journey
through
Depression*

JOHN H. TIMMERMAN

MULTNOMAH · PRESS

10209 SE Division Street, Portland, Oregon 97266

Edited by Deena Davis
Cover design by Bruce DeRoos

A SEASON OF SUFFERING
© 1987 by Multnomah Press
Portland, Oregon 97266

Multnomah Press is a ministry of Multnomah School of the Bible, 8435 NE Glisan Street, Portland, Oregon 97220

Printed in the United States of America

Library of Congress Cataloging-in-Publication-Data

Timmerman, John H.
   A season of suffering : one family's journey through depression / John H. Timmerman.
      p.   cm.
   Bibliography: p.
ISBN 0-88070-210-9 (pbk.)
   1.Depression, Mental.   I. Title.
RC537.T56 1987   616.85'27—dc19   87-30675
87 88 89 90 91 92 93 - 10 9 8 7 6 5 4 3 2 1

Contents

Foreword

Depression simply cannot be abstracted to a human condition and still be understood. It is a human experience first. One is subject to it even before one can subject it to definitions and analysis and explanations. First, we suffer—an astonishing number of us suffer—depression; and then, apart from the sufferance, we think about it; and then we prepare methods of sympathy and healing for others. Without that sense of the experience, the crucial element of human sympathy is missing, and all the medical or psychological analyses in the world are lacking.

John H. Timmerman has done a remarkable (but necessary) thing in his book, *A Season of Suffering*. Besides the excellent contemporary research which he offers on clinical depression (again and again taking me to a cool remove from the heat of the depressional drama), he gently invites me into the experience; he allows me to companion him through the personal event which he and his wife Pat suffered after the birth of their child

Joel. Never does he sentimentalize the experience. Never does the narrative slip to bathos. This narrator is in perfect control. Yet he is so particular and so immediate in his recounting of the memory, so clean, exact, and accurate in telling the tale, that I found myself a full participant. Most powerfully, he includes as a running counterpoint to his own description, Pat's journal notes, written during the history of her depression. Whereas John recreates the time and events for me, Pat overwhelms me with the rush of her own feelings—and I astonished myself, as I read her words, with sudden and very personal tears.

As much as human beings can teach one another of an experience which is frightfully private, the understanding of which is only now emerging with physiological research, John Timmerman teaches in this book about depression. As much as the Christian can realistically depend upon Holy Promises, upon others in the Holy Community, upon human knowledge and educated therapy, Timmerman carefully reveals in this book. The experience which he and Pat suffered together is unique to them, indeed. But Timmerman's art, specifically, makes it universal, more than a single example, an experience for every reader. And his uncomplicated explanation of the present medical knowledge regarding clinical depression makes his an extraordinary case-study, giving flesh to what otherwise would be scientific and abstract.

"Depression doesn't happen to one person alone," he begins the book. It is the experience of a family, he explains. By the time Pat returns home in the eighth chapter, when both husband and wife, parents and children step tentatively toward balance, and by the time the author writes his non-ending to his personal tale, that story has become our own, a chapter in the reader's own life. And the reader realizes that depression doesn't happen to one person alone—but is the experience of a whole community. The book itself has both sucked him in and then sent him forward, the wiser for the experience.

Walter Wangerin, Jr.

Acknowledgments

For the many friends who were with us during the dark hours, caring for us, reassuring us, and leading us in the peace of God, our deepest gratitude. And to Arnold and Peggy Knoll, to whom this book is dedicated, our thanks again.

According to thy word.
They shall praise Thee and suffer in every generation
With glory and derision,
Light upon light, mounting the saints' stair.

T.S. Eliot, *"A Song for Simeon"*

Preface

For too long a kind of mystery has cloaked the illness of depression. To understand it—physiologically, psychologically, and spiritually—the whole picture must be given. Not just that of the onlooker, wrapped in a shield of objectivity, cold medical terms, and some well-reasoned advice; nor just the ill person, subsumed in the dark sea of illness which seems impenetrable by encouragement, terms, or advice.

In a family, depression doesn't happen to one person alone. It happens to the whole family. Truly the person suffering from depression feels singled out and terribly alone. But that person is suffered with and for.

During her seven-week hospitalization for depression, my wife, Pat, kept a careful journal, an extension of her writing from happier times. When we as a family would travel, Pat kept a family journal which held those priceless, unforgettable moments fresh before us. When Pat underwent this illness, her journal included things we wish we could forget. Some of those moments are, nonetheless, given in this accounting. It is our hope that they will help others better understand the illness of depression, themselves as emotional beings, and their God as one who has made a path in the sea of despair.

We will consider four major questions about depression in this book. First, *What is it like?* Depression is a mystery to the sufferer. Each case of the illness is different because it afflicts the unique psychology of the individual. Yet there are certain general traits and patterns that can help us better understand what it is like to suffer the illness.

Second, *What is depression?* Only recently has medical science moved toward a consensus about the nature of the illness and its treatment. Although there is still wide disagreement on causes and treatments, the illness itself is more clearly understood, and beneficial treatments are emerging as the cloak of mystery is lifted from it.

Third, *What can others do about depression?* Some people still retain either an unnatural fear of the illness or a morbid secrecy about it. It is absolutely essential for the health of the afflicted person that the immediate family and the larger church family know how to care for the suffering individual and family.

Fourth, *How do we understand depression in the Christian life?* How can God allow this to happen to one of his children? This is a hard question, but as we discovered, the clearest answers arrive from having undergone the experience. Quick answers hardly suffice. One has to go through the sea to see God's path in it.

1   His Path Is in the Sea

Fall 1968.

The lake shore held that wild, eerie beauty that comes like a promise after Labor Day. Cottages have been boarded up against winter storms. Cottagers have left behind fast-disappearing traces of a full summer. An old tennis shoe half-buried against a clump of sandgrass. The charred debris of bonfires scattered by the wind. Bits of driftwood polished by the lake, played with by small hands, now rest discarded to the ebb and flow of the waves.

The season was slipping into autumn; vacationers had prepared against winter.

It was the quiet time at the lake shore. The wind still seemed to hold the sounds of children's laughter, even while the sands effaced their footprints in the ceaseless sweep of wind. And for a time, time itself seemed to linger between seasons as if savoring the quiet.

The trees at the crest of the dune, supple birch and poplar twisting among the pine, showed a blush of gold at their tips. The sky held that particular dazzling blue, fluffed by a few high clouds, that old timers call a "Michigan sky."

We had come here, Pat and I, to savor the quiet, the change of season, in a lingering embrace. For our lives, too, were in transition in this September of 1968, and it was good to have this quiet place.

I had just finished my master's degree, but had been less anxious about that than the letter I had awaited. Each day, coming home from classes, I would walk reluctantly yet nervously hurrying to the mailbox. We knew it was coming. Four appeals had been filed. All had been denied. It was a matter of time and time wouldn't hold still. Not for a draft notice in 1968.

I took comprehensive exams with my mind on another exam—the pre-induction physical I had taken a few weeks before. Others had called the physical test at Columbus, Ohio, the "zoo." Indeed. A zoo of human bodies being bent into impossible positions while white-suited doctors and aides poked and probed and jotted quick notes on pads and others herded us from one station to another. What struck me then was that the lines never seemed to end. Just bodies moving, no longer people. And so I waited—waited the letter announcing the results of the master's comprehensives with less apprehension than I waited the letter about the other exam. The university letter arrived first. I was one of 10 candidates, out of 109 who were examined, to be accepted into the Ph.D program starting that fall semester. The second letter arrived a few days later. I was also one of thousands of young men in that year to be drafted into the army. There would be no university that fall. It felt as if a hole had been carved into our lives, and that we had fallen into a void of uncertainty.

That was why we had come to the shore, that stretch of sky and sand and sea that we had loved since childhood. Friends of ours had a cottage high on a dune overlooking Lake Michigan. They were happy to wait a few weeks before closing it for the season. It was ours for a brief, unforgettable time in early September as we mentally ticked off the days to our parting.

Memories of the year and a half that followed—the induction, basic training, the year in Vietnam with its noise and stench, the shivering red earth, the intolerable heat in the festering Delta region—have faded. But one afternoon at the lakeshore remains clearly in my mind, unfolding bit by bit. It is as clear and sturdy before me as this old mahogany desk at which I write, the events of the day as detailed as the nicks in the grain, the chipped corners, the faded varnish.

It was the afternoon of a day Emily Dickinson described perfectly:

> There came a day at summer's full
> Entirely for me;
> I thought that such were for the saints,
> Where revelations be.

Pat and I had walked north along the shore. The day was cool enough for her to wear my jacket, sleeves flapping loosely around her wrists, the waist falling below the hem of her shorts. I wore the old blue cardigan sweater that she had bought for me in high school. It was one of her first gifts to me when our long friendship began to "turn serious." Appropriate to wear now. Friends had turned lovers and still remained best friends.

Now we were mindful of a long separation ahead, an abyss of the unknown, opening like jaws. But we determined to rejoice in the brief time we had. In that same poem, Dickinson wrote:

> The hours slid fast, as hours will,
> Clutched tight by greedy hands. . . .[1]

We were greedy for each other's love: greedy for time. We held on tight and felt time slip away, knowing that for all its passing it would not separate us from our love.

The shoreline twisted like an endless ribbon, gulls knitting stitches along sea and sand with noisy calls and swift dives. Mists held to the shoreline, then burned clean under the crisp sun. The waves formed a gentle lapping at the shore. The water shifted from shoreline-blue to a radiant blue-green at the drop-off.

Having grown up near the shore, we both knew how suddenly those waves could shift. In the space of an hour the waves could become rolling breakers, sign of stormy weather moving onto the lake from distant Wisconsin. Then the red flags flew at the public beaches. We recalled stories of how people had been swept away by undertow. Sometimes we would stand at the water's edge, feeling the crushing suck and ebb around tightened ankles. Then the sea was a danger. It was not surprising, then, as we headed back toward the cottage in the afternoon sun, that one of us remarked, "Storm's coming." The waves shifted northerly and formed slight crests. The afternoon sun wore a thin veil of white haze.

When the sun set that night it was through sheets of molten fire; the clouds that choked the western horizon thrust the sun's flame through long jagged sheets. Crimson fell into the lake, lay there in a growing sea of flame broken only by the rising chant of the waves and the white curl of the breakers.

We sat on the crest of the dune, looking down upon the water. We were alone in this world, watching God paint a seascape just for the two of us. We sat thanking him for it, caught in a rapture of awe.

As a boy I would sit by my father along one such dune and ask him, "Can I see Chicago, Dad?"

"If you look hard enough, you never know what you'll see," he had said. And now, having looked long, I had no trouble seeing God's path in the sea. The heavens declared the glory of God.

The wind had risen, lashing the pines along the dune. When the sun slid west at last, the air turned cold. We went inside to play Scrabble by the fireplace until bedtime.

It was deep night when Pat gently shook me awake.

"You have to see this."

Foggily awake, I was aware of a distant booming. I smelled hot chocolate in the cottage.

"What time is it?" I asked.

"Three in the morning."

"And you're hungry?"

"Come and see."

The distant storm that had awakened Pat unfolded beyond the window. The wind cut like the high whine of a saw through the pines. Far out over the water lightning dazzled in an unending dance. Jagged streaks charred through black clouds, illuminating the whole lake in leaping swells of wave. It was a volcanic fury, a glory of terrible proportions. For a moment the lake was a black void with only the scream of wind; then it erupted into a frothy glare as the lightning boiled.

We stood spellbound, sipping hot chocolate by the window, separated from the full storm only by shivering panes of glass.

I threw a few birch logs on the fireplace as we watched. Their hissing and snapping played a sharp counterpoint to the full-throated blast of the sea's roaring. At last the storm moved on shore, enveloping the cottage in its force. We sat safe and protected in the big room, the fire still snapping cozily.

We fell asleep on the couch before the fire and awakened late that morning to a world changed, all changed. Leaves and twigs littered the dunes. Here a shaggy old pine had been rived by lightning. There a section of dune caved in by the wash of rain, its gouge revealing huge roots awkwardly twisted before the new sun. The waves crashed against the shore, pounding it with white blows. The Coast Guard station had recorded waves fifteen feet high during the storm. And everywhere, in the shining cold air, in the waves, in the silver bottoms of beech leaves turning before the wind, was the cold bite of autumn.

But this thought was in our minds all day. *In the roar of the waters was a voice of majesty: Indeed, his path is in the sea.* The voice came to us then as a note of triumph. God has fashioned the sea; his way is in it. "Let the sea roar," says Isaiah (42:10). It doesn't matter, for the Lord "makes a way in the sea, a path in the mighty waters" (43:16). It was the kind of day when one revels in the majesty of God and in the glory of being a son or daughter of the Most High whose way is in the sea.

I hadn't thought of that verse—that truth—for a long time. Not until it was forced upon us in a way that shattered our hopes, until it became a plea, a prayer.

For the human mind can also become like the sea—a dark boiling mass lit by jagged streaks of raw lightning. The tempest roars, and there is no safe room to hide in, no fireplace to sit before. The world is lit by lightning, but the afflicted huddle in darkness. Indeed, there are times when one is *in* the sea, or the sea in that person; it is hard to tell the difference. One is only mindful of the billowing of black waves and the roar and then one casts out a thin lifeline of pleading prayer—his path is in *this* sea. And, still, one wonders.

It was a long time before that verse came back to us, and then with grinding urgency. The water was not sucking at our ankles. This time my friend, my beloved, my wife, was swept away in the undertow while I stood devastated on shore, unable to do little more than reach out a hand. And hope. And pray. That his way is in the sea.

To want something for a long time almost heightens our surprise when it finally comes to pass. We can't quite believe it has come true.

Perhaps we never outgrow our childhood in that way. And this is a good thing—this sense of longing, this wonder, this surprise when the longed for becomes the reality.

As Christians we live expectantly but not without surprise and wonder. The mystery of longing, of surprise, of wonder persistently infiltrates the Christian life, reminding us, in the words of a familiar catechism, "that we are not our own, but belong body and soul, in life and in death, to our Lord and Savior Jesus Christ."

And so we poise on a pinnacle between expectancy and wonder. At times we hardly dare to hope; at other times we wonder why we ever doubted. Such is the mystery of human nature.

This longing Pat and I had came to fulfillment in a sudden and unexpected way. It had been in our minds already during that autumn day at the lake shore. It had been there quietly expectant ever since. Understand this: both of us love children. Rather, God gave us a gift for loving children. Why then did we have to endure six years of waiting and countless medical exams before the first of our own arrived? Just remembering those fertility tests gives me a shiver of apprehension.

Here is a mystery.

After several years of trying to have children, this thought entered our minds one night—How about adoption? It was one of those sudden turnings of a page in the book of one's life: a turning that changes the story altogether. We were young at the time—no need for long, logical discussions. The impulse entered our minds with the suddenness of grace and we acted upon it, calling a local agency the next day to inquire about adoption. The formal procedures developed quickly, but occasionally with some embarrassment. There was the day when the caseworker visited our tiny, two-bedroom home. It had been immaculately cleaned, of course, in preparation for this "home visit." When the caseworker began inquiring about our finances, however, our faces fell blank. What finances? We lived on an undependable combination of my scholarship, some G.I. benefits, and Pat's work as a nurse. For the two of us, we thought we lived pretty high. When the caseworker totaled the annual amount however, the figure was startlingly small. We lived on that! Very well. How much in the bank? Nothing? We wore our naiveté in bewildered stares. But the mystery lies in the power of God's grace.

Nine months later, almost from the day of our first phone call, we held a nine-week-old baby boy in our arms. How young that couple looks in the polaroid photo taken at the agency as we held Jeffrey in our arms for the first time. It was one moment on a Thursday afternoon, one moment along the way of life, but also one that focused our lives eternally. Before that moment there were two: forever after there are three. A focus in time's turning by which we measure our lives.

Here is the second mystery.

After all the tests, all the discussions with fertility experts that had preceded the gift of Jeffrey, we knew thorough contentment. Imagine our surprise, then, when eleven months after we adopted Jeffrey our daughter Betsy was born. That two-bedroom house on the farm in southeastern Ohio grew suddenly smaller as it echoed now with the calls of children. The bedroom that had been my study stood wall to wall with cribs, a changing table that was seldom vacant, and a litter of toys. I moved my desk to a corner behind the washer and dryer, both of which seemed to be in use twelve hours a day. I completed my graduate studies listening to the beat of the washer, writing a dissertation to the rhythm of its gurgle and gush, and named this mystery grace.

Here is a third mystery.

We had moved to Pennsylvania, to one of those small towns where the most exciting event of the year is the Fourth of July parade when the new fire engine glistens down Main Street on the heels of the Baton Twirlers Corps. After the crowd dodges the flying batons and is honored by the creative thumping of the high school band, the children rush forward to receive suckers flung by the firemen from the new engine. Nothing much happens in such towns. One makes the most of small things. One has to think hard to remember the last crime. It may have been the time when the high school seniors broke into the church at midnight and set all the bells in the carillon tower howling. Down by the creek there is a football field where brown-haired Jeff and blond-curled Betsy could race their parents into weariness.

Slipped into that quiet time was the birth of our second daughter, Tamara. We thought she was the last. We were content with that understanding, and named the fullness of this lovingkindness a family. These mysterious blessings of God come each in his own time, by his grace.

We had moved now to Michigan.

Despite our quiet understanding that Tammy was to be our last, we still harbored a yearning to have another child. We wanted to adopt again. Times had changed radically in adoption procedures. We sent letters and made phone calls to agencies. We opened ourselves to whatever God would send us: the hard to place, the special need. Each letter seemed to get lost, go unanswered, or lead to a dead end.

I would watch my three growing children roar about the park across the street and confess, "My cup runneth over." And add, "enough is enough," when I saw Betsy in the middle of August parade around the swing sets in her mother's bathrobe, an old hat, and a pair of winter boots. She decorated the park. While Tammy paddled doggedly in the swimming pool, Jeff waged an intergalactic battle among the sycamore trees with some friends and dozens of dilapidated Star Wars figures.

The park across the street from our house is a wonderful roar of inner city action. Children's laughter careens above the pure noise of ghetto blasters and the crash of the basketball hoops, and for a time our three contributed their utmost to the furious swirl. So they grew, and in time outgrew the park. The years passed and they grew up.

My cup runneth over. But when are there ever enough cups to pour love into? And so God sent special children our way for short periods of time, children with needs that we could tend to in our home. As a matter of fact, this fourth mystery begins at a point when, in addition to our own three children, three more—Sarah, Kelli, and Richard (and he was more than one, this Richard!) were also living under the roof of our three-bedroom home.

Now, this is a small house we live in. The kind where you trip over bodies sprawled on the floor playing Monopoly, the kind where a never-ending litter of toys and dolls defies our best efforts at "housekeeping." Throw a dog, two hamsters, and a lethargic goldfish into it. What a sweet bellow of noise, shouts, laughter, and tears.

But what a rotten place to study. So the story begins in a bit of selfish need. Although I have an ample office at the college, it is hard to find a time when a student doesn't wait at the door. Besides, I have always liked to write at home. I was then working in a small study tucked away in the basement.

When I first presented the idea to Pat her eyes sort of went glassy. I knew what the answer would be. I had heard it when we bought our first house in Pennsylvania, a huge, old, lovely barn of a house that I had to strip down to its rudiments and rebuild. Perhaps this office idea wasn't quite as preposterous. Her expected response came out like this: "If you think you can?" That's a question, a challenge, a hesitation, and an affirmation all in one.

So it was that early June found the top half of our story-and a-half bungalow stripped away. An odd feeling that: opening the doorway to the upstairs and seeing sky. We prayed that it wouldn't rain while we laid roof trusses in place . . . working furiously from dark to dark to help the prayers along.

But the remodeled second floor, expanded to two huge bedrooms and a bath for the children, thereby freeing the second bedroom on the main floor for my study, went up surely, steadily, and rain free.

Pat was busy enough and patient enough not to notice the incredible mess. She had been a volunteer for the last year at the Christian Learning Center (CLC), a school for handicapped children a few blocks from our house. She helped in the classroom, romped with the kids on the playground at recess, and somehow bestowed order in a sea of loving kids who persisted in planting wet kisses on her at the oddest moments. During the summer months, while I stalked around in sawdust and plaster, she regularly attended planning meetings for the rapidly expanding CLC, while our own three children and others paraded along. Our house sometimes looked like a United Nations project both in children and its condition.

And so the summer of 1984 moved along to the snarl of power saws and the thunk of hammers, with the best saved for last. Lovingly I approached the now vacant bedroom on the main floor. In my basement study I have two tiny windows through which I can barely glimpse my neighbor's brown fence. Both of the windows are sealed shut. Here I would have two full-size windows, one overlooking the backyard flower garden, both opening to the breeze. While upstairs I had slammed walls and ceilings and wiring in place at a furious pace, working as long and hard as aching muscles would hold up, I worked in my new study with slow deliberation. Always there was the roar of children about, but I didn't mind. My own three were growing up. And I would have my study.

Carefully I framed the new built-in bookshelves out of top-grade lumber. There's something about the smell of a piece of new wood as the saw first bites into it that I love. I savored it now. I took special care with the trim moldings. In fact, I was outside staining the molding when Pat came around the corner of the house with the oddest, most radiant smile I can remember.

This moment of the fourth mystery is better told in Pat's journal during those weeks while I had puttered happily in my new . . . study?

August 13, 1984. I awaken at 5:30 A.M. and feel nauseated. This is the day Jeff has his foot surgery to correct some bone structures. Our alarm is set for 7 A.M. so Tim and I can be at the hospital by 8:30. I wonder how I'm going to make it since I feel like I'm coming down with the flu. Jeff's surgery goes well.

August 15. Jeff gets to come home this morning. He walks well with crutches but would like to stay at the hospital because of remote control TV.

August 18. While at the store today I checked out the pregnancy test kits. I didn't buy any. Why waste $9 when I couldn't be pregnant.

August 20. Last night I bought a home pregnancy test to do in the morning. Now I'm really wondering. Sarah, Richard, and Kelli are all here. I haven't mentioned it to Tim. He's working on the bookcases in his new study. I wonder how he will react if I am pregnant.

August 21. At 10 A.M. I ran the test and set it on the floor of the closet. I won't allow myself to check it until it's time in forty minutes. I sit down to have my devotions. I've prayed that God's way would be done. I find that I feel very excited and I'm praying that if it's negative I won't be too disappointed. At 10:40 I cautiously creep to the closet floor. I hardly dare to look at it. I catch a quick glimpse. There's a dark donut shape which means it's positive. I sit back on the floor and say, "Oh thank you, Jesus. This is a wonderful surprise." I sit alone, stunned, for ten minutes. I wonder, "Should I tell Tim now?" I'm so excited I can't wait. He's just finishing staining some bookshelf moldings. I can't remember exactly what I said. I think I asked him first, "What would you think if I were pregnant?" He just looked at me and smiled. Then I think I said, "Well, I am. There's a positive test inside." He thinks I'm teasing, but he knows I wouldn't joke about that. He looks stunned. We go inside and I show him the test. Tim is so sweet all day but very quiet.

August 23. Only one more day and Richard and Kelli will be going home. I'm just too tired to enjoy them. I made an appointment with the doctor.

August 26. It's our anniversary—18 wonderful years and now God is giving us one more blessing. It's only our secret still. Celebrating at Arnie's Restaurant is sweetly solemn. I think we still wonder if our news is true.

August 29. Tim and I join Jeff at City High School for his orientation. I'm suddenly conscious that I'm the only pregnant woman there. Everyone else looks so old.

August 30. *At 9:30 I see the doctor. The nurse takes my medical history and tells about the genetic counseling clinic at another hospital if I should want amniocentesis done. I assure her I'm not interested. She says anyone over 35 is considered high risk. If I weren't a Christian and feeling God's hand on my shoulder, I might worry about whether our baby is normal. I also asked the nurse if any of the five doctors in the office do abortions. She assures me, "No, they don't and never have." The bookkeeper stops by and tells me that five years ago she had a beautiful normal baby boy at the age of 37. That was nice of her. The doctor examined me. He can just barely feel my slightly enlarged, tipped uterus. As he left the room he smiled and said, "You did it up nice." I guess he said that because he could tell how happy I am to be pregnant. I think to myself, "Little baby, you're loved so much already."*

Pat wrote in her journal that I had a stunned smile when she told me the news. Actually, I was remembering, thinking back to those early days of our marriage when we had wondered if we would ever have children, and thinking how good God had been to us.

At the moment she told me, though, we wandered back into the uncompleted study.

"Yes, the crib had better go there in the corner. We still have a crib, don't we?"

We did, but it had been loaned out. Along with most of our other baby things. Loaned out or given away. Who would have expected that we would have a baby now? Now, with three children growing up? Now, at this age?

The reactions of the older children to this unexpected event were what one might expect. Thirteen-year-old Jeff greeted it with a grunt and went to his room to play a computer game. Twelve-year-old Betsy shrieked; not for joy as it turned out, but from embarrassment. Her mother pregnant! Eight-year-old Tammy gave us both a hug. The consensus was pretty much something like this: You guys got yourselves into this mess, don't look to us to help you out!

As it would turn out, their help became more than they, or we, ever expected.

2   In the Waves:
Help in a Time of Need

This business of having babies should be taken with a certain sense of humor. Especially if one joins a Lamaze class. We had done it this way for our other children and would for this one too.

The surprises started the first night when we showed up for class carrying the required pillows through a January snowstorm. Twelve couples and one unwed mother packed the teacher's living room. We were looking for one thing—a couple older than us! I had announced in passing to one of my classes, "Well, I'm going to be a daddy in my dotage." The students applauded! One girl stopped by after class to tell me her parents were expecting. So we weren't alone. But we were that night. Everyone sprawled around this living room, in various states of distention, looked so young! Well, we felt young. Weren't we having a baby?

With our baby, Joel, now an active preschooler, we still furtively look around at other parents. We discover we're not alone after all. The park across the street is

packed with young children churning through the wading pool, tumbling over bars like little monkeys, erecting
clumsy castles in the sandbox. We stop every so often
while Joel roars along with the rest of them, and eye the
parents. Surprise: Many couples are having children later
in life. Is that a father or a grandfather? I'll never ask.
For the first time—today—as I take a break from writing
this chapter, a man asks me the unforgivable question,
"Your grandson?" I laughed out loud. Oh, how I've
waited for that. And when he asked I couldn't think of
a clever comeback. "No," I said, "my son." And that
was enough. Because of our age, however, we took this
business of birth exercises and preparation seriously.
While these youngsters at the class loafed through their
exercises, we broke a sweat after five minutes. One of
our tennis partners used to exclaim after a hard match,
"Doesn't it feel good to sweat!" I would whisper the line
during deep breathing exercises and we would crack up,
laughing among a floor full of pregnant bodies and bewildered stares.

But it paid off. We both like to keep in shape, and
seldom had we been in better shape than for this delivery. We had a kind of giddy joyfulness through the whole
waiting period. Each night around the dinner table we
tried out names with the other children. "That does it,"
I would say when we disagreed, "if it's a boy it's Elmer
Claude."

"And if it's a girl, Daddy?" Tammy would ask.

"Elmira Claudia, of course."

And Tammy would bury her face in a groan. "Oh,
Daddy. No!" Of course we knew—we were the experienced pros—that each birth is different. Betsy gave about
eighteen hours of hard labor. Tammy was induced and
fairly exploded into the world. This one would break all
records.

Pat awakened me at about 4:00 A.M. "I think it's time, but no hurry."

"Okay. I'll have a bowl of cereal first."

A few minutes later she stepped out of the shower and said, "Maybe you'd better hurry."

"Okay, I'll get the car out."

And as we drove out the driveway, "I think you had better really hurry." How nice, I thought, as I gunned the car down the empty streets, to have three children old enough to take care of themselves when Mom and Dad have to leave during the night.

I dropped Pat off at the emergency entrance and by the time I had parked the car and raced up four flights of stairs, I found a frantic nurse trying to attach something called an external heartbeat monitor to Pat's rapidly changing middle.

"Oh, dear," said the young nurse. "I'm supposed to get this. Oh, dear. I don't have time."

I think we had been through this more often than the nurse. I said to Pat, "Let's get down to the birthing room. Even if I have to carry you myself."

I barely had time to scrub and get in a mask and gown in the birthing room. And then—red light. All of a sudden baby decided to take a snooze. Enough work. Brake time, folks.

We laughed at first. Then groaned. Then waited. The doctor sat wearily twirling an instrument.

"Well, you'll have to work after all, " he said.

And Pat did. But an hour later Joel Mark placed his judgment upon the world by one look and a forceful pronouncement on the state of mortal affairs. I'm sure he woke up patients on the far side of the hospital. His tiny mouth opened until it looked like the Grand Canyon. His face turned a deep red. And he exploded, erupted, in a glorious squall of indignation.

"This is no Cabbage Patch doll," I murmured in awe.

"He has lungs that'll rock the fourth floor," the doctor agreed. Indeed he did. But what a thrill to hear it.

There are two things in this world that take too much time: giving birth and having parents talk about giving birth. Suffice it to say that Joel Mark arrived on the scene in God's own time.

There were some minor ailments in those early days of post-birth. For example, Joel was jaundiced with a slightly elevated bilirubin count (the result of the immature liver's inability to expel waste), but nothing severe. Tammy had spent five days under the ultraviolet lights for a severely elevated bilirubin count after birth and was scheduled for a transfusion when the bilirubin miraculously cleared in a matter of hours. This seemed no more than a minor inconvenience. A bit more serious was the fact that Pat suddenly developed thrombophlebitis on her lower leg. Motrin, an anti-inflammatory drug, was prescribed. She had to keep her left leg elevated. Another inconvenience, we thought. Nothing serious.

Except in retrospect. It should have been a caution to us. Any physical abnormality following birth warrants attention.

Other signals lighted up as we moved home. Philip Yancey has written a fine essay called "In Defense of Pain," collected in his book *Open Windows*. Yancey points out, through examples from Dr. Paul Brand's rehabilitative work with sufferers of leprosy, that pain is a warning system God has blessed us with. Pain—who wants it? Nobody. But consider life without it. Yancey writes, "By definition, pain is unpleasant, so unpleasant as to *force* us to withdraw our finger from boiling water, lightning-fast. Yet it is that very quality which saves us from destruction. Unless the warning signal demands response, we might not heed it."[2] Nobody wants pain; but we cannot live long without its warning system.

The trouble is, we ignore the warnings. This second signal warned us of danger in what was becoming a swiftly confusing spiral. Pat's postpartum bleeding lasted several weeks. After a physical, her gynecologist prescribed methergine (*Methylergonovine Maleate*), a drug used to stop excessive bleeding. Clearly something was amiss—a blood clot, excessive bleeding. But to the uninitiated, no clear physiological indication of danger. Just little painful reminders of something not quite right. Her increasing tiredness was also attributed to this. The delicate dance of maternal hormones was awry; it was natural to be tired. But why, then, the inability to sleep? Tired people need rest, but how does one rest when one can't sleep?

We are now quite aware of the fact that the three danger points for the onset of depression for women are pre-menstrual syndrome, postpartum, and menopause. We are also aware that nearly twice the number of women as men are subject to depression of the type Pat experienced.

For Pat's tiredness, too, there seemed to be logical explanations (ah, how the mind reaches for *reasons*). Joel was born in mid-April, just when I was beginning to conclude my courses at the college—trying to surface from a sea of papers, trying to prepare, administer, and grade final exams. I dropped further and further from the nurturing role of father. And more and more of the burden shifted to Pat.

Again, hindsight proves effective. Would it have been so difficult to arrange some kind of day care in the home? Some part-time help to pick up part of the burden? No, of course not. We just didn't see the need. We did what we had always done. Exams had always come at this time. There had always been more pressure on mom during those days. It was routine, expected. And, I might add in retrospect, a key area in which to feel the crushing weight of guilt. Every depressed person feels an acute sense of guilt for not being able to cope with routine affairs. And every family feels guilt for not having re-routed those routine affairs. This is surely one of the most potentially destructive side effects of depression in the family.

But now it gets complicated. Almost six months prior I had agreed to teach the first session of summer school, which started only a few days after the regular school session. I was on a roller coaster rocketing out of gear. Normally that wouldn't faze us. Our family was accustomed to the quirks and demands and pressures of college teaching. But those pressures were accentuated by another irregularity. Joel developed a colic condition so severe that our pediatrician prescribed Levsin PB (a compound of a muscle relaxant from the Belladonna alkaloids, and the sedative Phenobarbital)—a rather potent, but not infrequently prescribed, drug for colic.

Hearing the ingredients, we protested to the doctor, "But we don't like to give medicines unless there's a strong need."

He looked at us wisely, and murmured, "*You* need it. Both of you." That was true. But it's a hard reason to give a medicine to a child to salvage your own nerves.

Here is the pattern, then, that has become so terribly familiar to others afflicted with depression. Bit by bit you feel yourself slipping from routine patterns, the commonplace by which we measure health in our lives. Feeling that norm slip away, you begin to fight back, believing you can regain it by your own strength. Now surely there are many such events in the life of a family whereby you can do so. Life simply doesn't always go on an even footing; there's always some slipping and sliding and pressure. Quite often we weather those uneven spots admirably; order is restored in time, the commonplace regained. Such is the normal pattern. And such is the

reason why we avoid seeking help when the fight becomes overwhelming. We tend to think that if we can
just hold out a little bit longer, everything will be all
right. Even when it's going all wrong.

As those weeks headed into summer school, we both
sensed a kind of desperation hovering in the air. Like a
black bird of prey, it seemed to have its claws poised.
The weariness became etched in Pat's face, and I hoped
she wouldn't see the weariness in mine. We tried to get
away—a dinner out here, some shopping there. It only
reminded us how harried we were getting.

We were grateful for little achievements, like Joel's
quiet behavior during his baptism, or during his brother's
honors assembly. But the little achievements were merely
reprieves for an hour.

About a week before the summer school ended, Pat's
gynecologist encouraged her to wean Joel to a bottle.
Perhaps this would help the still unsettled hormonal
imbalance achieve order. I found myself praying desperately—help me make it through one more week, Lord.
Then I can take over. My last class is on Monday; the
exam Tuesday. Then we're free.

Weeks before, I had bought tickets for myself and the
three older children to a weekend Tigers baseball game.
I bought these just a few days after Joel was born, thinking that with mom and dad's energy going to the baby,
the older ones would need some special attention.

But now I also became increasingly aware of a greater
need at home. Would Pat be able to take care of the baby
while we were gone for the day? The very question was
unsettling. She could take care of anything, under normal circumstances. Now she was increasingly afraid to
be left alone. I could read the silent pleading in her eyes.
On Thursday night I used the phone in my study and
called some friends to offer them the tickets. I went back
upstairs much relieved.

"Don't worry about it, honey," I said. "I want to give the tickets to the Vanden Bergs. They'll go."

"Are you sure?"

"I've already taken care of it."

"I don't want to be alone," Pat said. And she was crying with the thought, with her uncontrollable weakness.

This is the same woman who had always been as independent as a summer day. It was her idea to live in a basement apartment in a seedy section of Brooklyn for the six weeks of training I had there before going to Vietnam. "Hey, God will take care of me," she had said. That was good enough for both of us. God did. We saw each other every possible hour during those six weeks. And it was from that little apartment that she drove me, through a howling February blizzard, to Fort Dix to catch my flight to Vietnam while she drove on to Michigan in our battered Buick through that same blizzard. This was one tough lady, my wife. And now she sat crying at the thought of a few hours of absence. Lord, what's happening?

By the weekend she trembled if I left the house at all. She came to bed at night, but did not sleep. I sensed her lying there quietly, not sleeping. Three nights passed that way.

I had to teach that Monday. If only I could make it through I could get someone to proctor the exam. When I left the house I knew I wouldn't make it through.

By 10:00 A.M. the office phone rang while I was taking a break . . . or breaking down, head in my hands, throwing desperate pleas to God.

"Tim," said my mother-in-law, "I think you had better come home."

"Yes. Yes, I know." With a shiver I packed my briefcase and hurried home.

Remember your dreams from childhood—the ones that stay with you a lifetime? Good dreams and bad dreams walked at their choosing through the young mind.

Perhaps one was a sweet dream of mountain meadows, splashed with flowers. The grass spreads in a lush green so rich it is like liquid. Overhead a clear blue sky. Maybe it's a glimpse of our own longing, such good dreams. Maybe a glimpse of heaven.

And then there were the unforgettable bad dreams. We try to bury those. Yet they pop up like bad weeds. Some of those bad dreams I can remember as if they were occurring now. Reality fades. Present slides into past and so is done, leaving its imprint to be sure, but events shift and change. Reality is the accustomed, the commonplace, the blessing of order. Bad dreams are the impingement of disorder, the abhorrent, the feared dislocation of the commonplace.

It is that old dream of falling. No one reaches out to stop the terrible, swift plunge. Only the falling; if only you could hit bottom. Or, it is that corridor of rooms from which there seems to be no way out. Some *presence* lurks out there, stalking you. But all the rooms are dead ends. There is no exit, no safe arms to cling to. Or, again, it is that leering face, indistinct but threatening, that waits horribly at every turn.

We try to bury those dreams. They are only dreams, after all. Go away! Don't bother me! And in our reality we escape to safe arms.

For the depressed person there are no safe passages. Now the dream becomes the reality—the tossing, the falling, the locked-in feeling. A sea of darkness rolls up, and the mind—that fragile little network of chemicals and fibers—spins helplessly out of control.

There are as many contributing causes to depression as there are individual experiences. And as many kinds of depression as there are individual lives. It is unique to each individual who undergoes it. It is the most intensely personal illness there is, for its very nature is to invalidate the sufferer of any sense of self-worth or self-esteem, to deny the sufferer his or her self. "This is not I," the depressed person wants to cry out. Just so. The "I" is lost in a sea of crashing waves.

Sometimes words simply fail us when we are asked to describe something of deep significance. This failure can have its amusing effects. We have all experienced those embarrassing moments when, by a slip of the tongue, we say what we don't mean.

Our language, after all, is anything but an exact medium for meaning. Usually that meaning comes through by tones, gestures, and emphasis as well as the words themselves.

At other times, however, we may experience an event so unfathomable as to beggar the descriptive ability of language. Words seem either too impressive or too exact. They fail to contain *this* event in our minds or experience. Such experiences may be the ecstasy of joy or the numbness of grief. Then again, they can be events like depression.

Emily Dickinson's short poem on pain somehow probes the experience of depression better than all the scientific terms in the world:

> *Pain has an element of blank;*
> *It cannot recollect*
> *When it began, or if there were*
> *A day when it was not.*
>
> *It has no future but itself,*
> *Its infinite realms contain*
> *Its past, enlightened to perceive*
> *New periods of pain.*[3]

In the brief moment of this poem, Dickinson seizes the quality—the experience—of depression. That experience also bears its element of blankness. Pat would find it most difficult to say how her depression started, where it began. In retrospect, certain signs could be cited; but it seems that suddenly depression *was* the state of being for her. She could not remember a time when it was otherwise except, perhaps, as an impossibly remote event. Also, she found it hard to envision a time when it would not be like this. Depression robbed her of the sense of past, and the hope of a future that might be different. That's what depression is: an attenuated present which seems incapable of changing.

Despite its intensely personal nature, certain general characteristics typify depression. The difficulty here is detecting some of the signals that depression is occurring or is at risk. The first lesson Pat and I learned is that we waited too long to get help. And yet this is understand-able, and is in fact quite typical of the experience of depression.

Consider an analogy. Let's say that you are suddenly transported to a wholly different country from any you have ever known before. Or even imagine another world, for indeed, depression is another world, not just a for-eign but related land. You arrive in this other world without any benefit of markers or signs to map the ter-rain. As you wander into the land, you believe that what-ever happens to you is simply strange, but not necessar-ily threatening, not necessarily a cause for fear. You have accustomed things with you—a sun rises and sets, you see people you know (even if they all seem to be walking away from you). But then suddenly you discover that the path you have been traveling has gotten more strange. It seems to slope downhill and you feel hurried down the slope. Terrifying things occur. You see things you never dared imagine before. Voices speak horrible things to you and you don't know where the voices come from. You can no longer remember the way out. The path slides downhill into a pit. You claw at the smooth walls, but the sand you tear loose only showers down upon you, burying you in the pit.

Then you look back and wish that someone had posted signs: Danger Ahead! Stop Here! Get Help!

The keenness of retrospect, of experience, knows where those danger points lie. Experience of the horrible sliding into the pit tells us where we should have done things differently. So too there are certain danger signals for depression.

Any one of these is not necessarily a pattern which means that depression is inevitable. Indeed, strange beings that we humans are, some of us can weather many of the signs and still not become ill with depression. Yet, we do well to heed the cautions. Imagine that it is a winter day, ten below zero, a biting wind whipping the snow. One person can walk outside without a coat for thirty minutes without getting chilled and ill. Another might get chilled in thirty seconds. Either of the two is foolish if they wear no coat at all, if they recognize no limits at all.

In our own situation, we found in retrospect a terrible pattern which seemed to lead unavoidably to the illness. A blood clot in itself will not cause depression. Nor, in itself, will extensive postpartum bleeding, even with the hormonal imbalances signaled by it and the administration of the drug, methergine. Nor, in itself, will the stress of a busy household and a colicky baby. These were all *contributing factors* in our case . . . none an isolated cause.

Such reflections whirled through my mind when I admitted Pat to the psychiatric hospital that evening in June. During the admission procedure one other very important contributing factor came into the picture. We had hardly been aware of it until the admitting psychiatrist elicited a medical history. On both the maternal and paternal sides of Pat's family there had been an extensive pattern, through three generations, of the women suffering mental disorders, chiefly of depression. Clearly there was a genetic disposition affecting the females of the family. But, once again, this in and of itself did not necessarily *cause* her depression.

The point here is that there are contributing factors and certain signs of which one should be aware. What signs? How can one tell when one needs help? How can one avoid the mistake—our first lesson—of waiting too long to get help?

Clinical analysis of signs and symptoms for depression generally divides these into four major areas of assessment.

1. *Affective Signs* include states of feeling, ranging from mild "blues" to severe despair. The depressed person feels some degree of anxiety and worry, anger, confusion, and hopelessness. Not all of these moods need be present, and they may range in degree. For example, some may experience anxiety in the form of worry—that things may go wrong during the course of the day. Others, such as Pat, may feel it so acutely that they feel incapable of handling even routine tasks and are terrified at the prospect of being left alone.

2. *Cognitive Thought Process Signs* are the ways in which the patient thinks about him or herself, and about relationships with others or situations. Problems with concentration and decision making occur. Typically, the depressed person has a very low self-esteem and feels incapable of clear decisions. The patient seems to have little control over thought processes, with thoughts of death or suicide intruding. In more severe

states, the patient may hear voices saying he or she is of no worth, should commit suicide, that life is hopeless. Generally, thinking processes become very confused and agitated.

3. Both of the above may be seen in *Behavior Signs*, which measure a person's actions. Because of low self-esteem and confused thinking, the depressed person may become terribly dependent and submissive. The patient may be fearful of being left alone, and desperately needs someone nearby, someone to take control. At the same time, the person may give in to relentless crying and withdrawal. She is often quite aware of the distance between her current feelings and thoughts and what she remembers as normal feelings and thoughts. The agitation of this conflict may give way to restless behavior such as pacing, trembling, and handwringing. Speech and action may become impeded. Routine activities, such as picking up the mail, reading the newspaper, or making coffee, may be forgotten. The patient loses a sense of pleasure in formerly pleasurable activities. For example, the patient may suddenly hate certain songs or hymns, a television program, flowers from the garden. Such things are associated with the person before the depression and, now hating oneself, the patient's low self-esteem rejects those formerly pleasurable activities.

4. Depression inevitably takes its toll upon *Physical Functions*. It has physiological as well as psychological effects. Initially, these symptoms may appear as a lack of energy, which may spiral rapidly into acute fatigue as sleep habits are disturbed. The patient may suffer physical symptoms such as constipation or diarrhea, indigestion, nausea, and headaches. Often, and despite the longing for physical contact, sexual patterns may be disturbed as the patient withdraws.

The patient often wants to be held or consoled, but lacks the focus of energy and will for sexual relationships.

Depression is often accompanied, furthermore, by physical signs. Since depression seems to affect the *triangularis*, or depressor muscles, which control the movement of the sides of the mouth, one might observe a down-turned angle to the lips. Posture is often affected, the patient characteristically appearing slouched, with shoulders bent forward as if a weight were pressing upon them. Eyes appear dull and listless, seeming to turn inward with kind of a glazed look from the inward pain. In few medical cases is the relation between mind and body more pronounced.

The symptoms described here, based largely on the *Diagnostic and Statistical Manual of Mental Disorders* published by the American Psychiatric Association[4], are given on a gradient from mild to severe. Some or all of the signs may signal clinical depression. Additional guidelines (see Appendix, question 6) enter into a clinical assessment of depression. For example, the depressed person typically interprets present experience in a negative way, views the past as absent of any achievement, and sees no possible alleviations in the future. Some or all of these signs may signal clinical depression. But, also, some of these symptoms are a part of everyday living. We all have days when we feel "blue." We all have days when we don't seem to concentrate clearly or we lack energy, or have nights when we don't sleep well. When do we seek help?

In an article entitled "Depressed or Just Discouraged?" psychologist Mary Vander Goot responds to the question "What's the difference between normal depression and depressive illness?" She writes:

Drawing a clear line between normal mood changes and depressive illness can be tricky, but it is possible to identify certain times when many people experience what could be called "mild depression." One such time is after a physical illness. Another is after a time of unusual stress; students, for example, sometimes feel a letdown after completing their final exams. Sometimes mild depression can follow a time of excitement or emotional intensity: you come back from a wonderful vacation and feel "down" about getting back into the routine; or you feel strangely depressed after a splendid Christmas reunion with your brothers and sisters. Such mild depression is usually not a cause for concern.[5]

But, Vander Goot further distinguishes, more serious events can have a more profound impact upon our lives:

Bereavement after the loss of a loved one may very well take the form of depression. A heavy mood, times of crying, and even some physical symptoms such as loss of appetite and sleeplessness are considered normal when they occur within the first year after the loss.[6]

These are expected patterns in human living, however. Depressive illness occurs when the expected patterns are overwhelmed by the illness itself.

As a general guideline, when an individual experiences symptoms detailed in the list of *Affective Signs, Cognitive Thought Process Signs, Behavior Signs, and Physical Function Signs* for a period of two weeks, help should be sought. The clearest signs to be alert to include the following:

—persistent feelings of guilt, sadness, and hopelessness,
—thoughts of suicide,

—poor concentration,
—changes in appetite,
—changes in sleep patterns,
—decreased interest in sex,
—loss of interest in daily activities.

The caution is to seek help early, rather than wait too long. But where does one go for help?

Assuming now that the afflicted person recognizes the personal need for help, four alternatives emerge.

The first is to seek the advice of a pastor. The best seminaries now routinely tutor pastors in psychological as well as spiritual counseling. A common pattern has been developed for such counseling. The pastor will see a person for four to six visits. If the problem seems insolvable within that space of time, the pastor should refer the person to other resources.

In less severe forms of depression—anxiety over daily problems, a persistent feeling of being "blue"—pastoral counseling can help tremendously. Since depression for the Christian inevitably raises spiritual concerns—a sense of being forsaken by God, for example—pastoral counseling is vital. Because the depressed Christian will have spiritual questions, the pastor should be involved in all further levels of help. Very rarely, however, does the pastor have the extensive psychological expertise necessary for prolonged therapy. However necessary the pastor's role, it should be recognized that depression is a medical illness and requires professional care.

The *clinical psychologist* enters the picture here. The psychologist may practice independently or be affiliated with a group or with a counseling agency. Some of these agencies may specialize in depression-related disorders, family or marital counseling, or drug abuse, for example. Depending on the needs of the patient, the psychologist will be able to offer varying forms of testing and therapy that are very beneficial for less severe forms of depression. Where a chemical imbalance is indicated, or medical prescriptions needed, the psychologist will generally refer the patient to a psychiatrist.

The *psychiatrist* is a medical doctor who has completed advanced training known as a residency in psychiatry. The importance of the psychiatrist and pharmaceutical treatment of depression has become increasingly important in recent years as medical science has become more informed about the chemistry of the brain during depression. Ages ago, the depressed person was commonly considered as simply being odd, different, unusual— someone with "problems." A few decades ago, such a person was commonly considered to have some difficulties that had to be talked out, yet he or she seldom dared talk about it! One still runs into this. During Pat's hospitalization a woman stopped me after church services. The congregation had prayed for Pat's healing. The woman inquired about Pat's condition and left me with the remark, "Well, we all have some problems, don't we?" Depression is an illness, not a "problem."

More recently, however, the majority of depression illnesses have been linked to biochemistries of the brain, a fact that will be discussed more fully in chapter three. An article in *Discover* magazine put the situation like this: "Delicate chemical networks in the brain that regulate thoughts and emotions as well as basic physiological processes are being mapped with increasing precision, and that knowledge is being used to develop customized drugs for different kinds of depression."[7] Two basic implications arise from this. First, depression isn't the result of anything the patient has done, nor the result of "problems." This is an essential understanding, for nearly all depressed persons will feel an acute sense of guilt, as if they have done something to cause the illness or as if they were responsible for it. Secondly, it implies that depression is an illness that can often be effectively treated with chemical means, that is, by use of medicines. The psychiatrist is able to diagnose this need and to prescribe medicines that effectively work to restore this biochemical equilibrium.

We have found among some Christians a tragic fear of such pharmaceutical treatment for mental illnesses. "Drugs" is a nasty word for them. As with all medical skill, we must see this also as a blessing, a means of God's effective healing.

When a depressed person is unable to function in the home or work place, when the person's illness is severe, or when thoughts of suicide increase—often occurring as the patient begins to feel that he or she is of no worth, hospitalization may be required. In the psychiatric hospital, the patient will be treated by a team headed by a psychiatrist, and including nurses, social workers, and psychologists. Increasingly, independent professional teams function in the same way. Such independent professional services may include a psychiatrist who administers therapy and prescribes a course of drug treatment, a psychologist who may administer therapy to both the patient and the patient's family and who oversees clinical testing, and a social worker, who will be responsible for taking a family history and administering certain kinds of diagnostic testing.

A block away from us lives a woman who began to become profoundly depressed during menopause. For three years she refused treatment, gradually isolating herself until she became a virtual captive of her own house. A neighbor who knows Pat and the treatment she received visited with her. She found the woman standing in the middle of her kitchen, palms pressed to her head, moaning relentlessly. Within hours she had talked the woman and her husband into admission at the same hospital where Pat was treated. Within six weeks the woman was able to return to normal life. "I just didn't know help was available," she said. "I thought I was alone in this."

One of the most common facets of the illness of depression is that the sufferer feels so terribly alone.

Help *is* available for the depressed person. However, the first step must be taken by the person or family. Sometimes a few sessions with a sympathetic listener can be therapeutic. But often professional expertise is necessary and must be sought. It is high time we strip away the myths surrounding depression—the myth that someone just has "problems," that someone is just "blue," that the afflicted person is somehow guilty and deserving of the "punishment." Only when we strip away those diabolical myths can we begin to understand the illness for what it is—an *illness*—and one treatable and curable by professional and divine help.

3 Adrift in the Sea: Identifying the Enemy

I t is 10:00 P.M. and I'm trying to put Joel to sleep. He does this sleeping magnificently in my arms, even with a healthy snore. But each time I lay him in the crib he squirms and awakens.

How did Pat do this?

I had put our other kids to bed when they were babies. I remember reading long stories to Jeff and then making up stories about people we would invent. Then he always fell asleep. That was so long ago. That's right, I sang to them. Strange that when I sing now they groan. Maybe they fell asleep to shut out the noise. Let's see . . . *Jesus loves me.* . . .

Joel doesn't like my singing. His eyes go wide, wider. That's not the idea. Very well, we'll walk. After ten laps around the house, having said good night to each flower, each star, and our yawning dog, Joel is carrying on learned discourse with the moon.

Standing outside in the back yard while Joel babbles at the moon, I see the light wink out in the girls' room.

Did I remember to say good night to each of them? Can they begin to understand this hole which has suddenly opened in their world?

Well, let's try the bottle again. Ah, he's dozing. I think we've got it this time. Then . . . the back door slides open quietly. Footsteps gingerly cross the kitchen. Okay, burglar. Take what you want and get out. Only be quiet!

It's our pastor. He sits down quietly across from me. It is enough to sit together that way for a while. I know he understands our pain. A member of his own family has battled this black illness, this illness that Winston Churchill called "the black dog."

He begins to talk quietly, easily. We are friends. There is no sham between us. I hurt; he knows it and ministers to it.

Then he says, "You know, there will be times when you will be angry with God."

Whoa, there, I think. I really don't think so. But I don't say anything. How true his insight will prove to be weeks, months ahead when each new turn in this hard road comes to a dead end. No, not angry with God. I'll be honest. I would become furious with God. "You could have stopped this," I would cry out. "You could have healed Pat. Now, Lord! Do your thing. Turn this around." But that night I said nothing, while Joel's little body relaxed and the snoring started. Funny how babies snore. What peace. What contentment.

"And that will be all right," our pastor was saying, "because God understands us. But he has also given us promises, and I want to give you this one." From memory, he spoke the words of Isaiah 43:1-3:

> But now thus says the LORD,
> he who created you, O Jacob,
> he who formed you, O Israel:
> "Fear not, for I have redeemed you;
> I have called you by name, you are mine.

When you pass through the waters I will be with you;
   and through the rivers, they shall not
      overwhelm you;
when you walk through fire you shall not be burned,
   and the flame shall not consume you.
For I am the LORD your God,
   the Holy One of Israel, your Savior."

Interesting passage. It does not say that we will never go through the fire, never pass through the waters. The promise is that when we do, we will not be consumed or overwhelmed by them.

And then he quoted one more verse, again from memory. They had been inscribed on his heart. This was from Isaiah 41:10.

Fear not, for I am with you,
   Be not dismayed, for I am your God;
I will strengthen you, I will help you,
   I will uphold you with my victorious right hand.

Not consumed, not overwhelmed because God upholds us with a victorious hand.

The passage didn't sink in right away. There was too much turmoil in my own mind. How many phone calls had I made during the frenetic passage of that day? First to the psychiatric hospital.

"I'm sorry, we won't have a bed free until Thursday," the admissions receptionist had said. What? How can this be? What shall I do? Then began a string of intervention calls to Pat's gynecologist. Yes, he was well aware of the difficulties and dangers.

"Can Pat function for a few more days?" he asked.

"No, I don't think so."

This was a wise man. He didn't offer any quick cure-alls, no "take two aspirin and call me in the morning." The morning! Would it come?

He would do what he could, he said. By 6:00 P.M. a

bed at the hospital had mysteriously appeared. But what a hollow, lost feeling we had as we drove to the hospital. Still, it was a lovely place, a kindly place if one can believe that. Flowers lined the walk to the front door. A soft breeze played among pine trees that gave the hospital its name: Pine Rest. How can the world be so sweet when my world is falling apart? I glanced sidelong at Pat and read the fear in her eyes. How did she see it? Here are her words:

Tuesday, June 18, 1985. (Joel will be 9 weeks tomorrow) Today I awakened with Joel at 7:45 A.M. I took a shower while he played in his crib. I slept terribly last night. I slept from 10:15 until Tim came to bed. Around 3:00 A.M. I became really agitated. I couldn't relax and felt like I had to vomit. I couldn't stand to hear the birds sing this morning.

At 8:30 A.M. while giving Joel his bottle, I started to tremble. I felt afraid to take care of him. Mom called and I told her I was depressed. At 10:30 she came over and I told her how awful I felt. I wanted Tim by me. I can't stop crying, and feel I'm going crazy. Tim had me lie in bed all afternoon. I feel so sad to see how sad I've made everyone. The girls are crying. At 6:00 P.M. Tim admitted me to Pine Rest. I feel relieved that there will be help. The admitting doctor tells me I will get well but I can't believe him. I can't stop crying. I've let so many people down. Right now the only relief I can feel is from Tim's love. At 9:30 I'm given some medicine to sleep. I haven't eaten all day.

The admitting psychiatrist at the hospital interviewed us together. From the start both of us were involved in all the steps. When depression afflicts one member of a family, it afflicts the whole family. This much I understood, and more, after he completed his diagnostic interview and we accompanied Pat to the ward where she would stay.

"We will be doing more tests, of course," the doctor

cautioned. And then he began informing us about this illness we knew so little about. "If you're like most people . . ." he was saying, and immediately that brought a strange sense of comfort. Yes, others had coped with this before. We're not all alone then. And these people around us, these doctors and nurses and therapists knew what to do. "If you're like most people, you're probably wondering how this happened. It's really difficult to tell at this point. Generally we distinguish external factors as one kind of cause."

Briefly he outlined relational causes, those occurring when we can't get along with others. Sometimes a relationship with a family member, an employer, or employee, can cause such acute anxiety that one becomes depressed, feeling incapable of any worth or good. Furthermore, there are situational causes or circumstances that can lead to depression. A death of a loved one, a broken friendship, a divorce, drug abuse, financial difficulties might be such situations—situations where things go all wrong and there seems to be no way out. But the second kind of depression, he was saying, is caused by internal factors. Then we have what we commonly call biologic depression.

"But," he pointed out, "those distinctions between external factors and internal factors are really too simple. Understand that I'm not trying to give you the whole picture here at one sitting. But it is true that chemical imbalances figure in nearly all forms of depression sooner or later. The odd thing we have here with Pat is that it seems to be nearly exclusively biologic.

"The genetic disposition is the first clue," he said. "You have depressive episodes in your mother and your maternal grandmother, in your paternal grandmother, and in two paternal aunts. Second, the postpartum period has clear indications—the blood clot, the prolonged bleeding—which would indicate a hormonal dysfunction. Third, your relationships with others seem wonderful. If I understand you correctly, you have good friends, a supportive family. And last, while any new-born causes some stress, I want to state categorically that the home situation is not a cause. No. Your depression would have occurred even if your baby never cried a peep and slept twenty hours a day. Your depression seems to be wholly biologic. We will, of course, do more testing in the next few days, but offhand I can say this. It is at once the worst of news and the best of news. Biologic depression can be the most severe depressive disorder. That's the bad news. But the good news is that since it's free of relational and situational problems, it is the most easily treated medically. Why, I would expect you to be back home in two to three weeks. The average hospitalization here for depression is about twenty-five days."

Bad news and good news. The follow-up testing would confirm the diagnosis, officially stated as a "severe major biologic depression." The bad news was that the two weeks would stretch into three, then four, then seven full weeks of hospitalization.

I had a compulsion to know, to understand, to identify this enemy that had invaded my household. All I saw were the effects of its malevolent forays, the devastating psychological destruction it worked. I didn't know the enemy.

Imagine that you awakened this morning to find your garage ransacked. The door is broken open. Bicycles are gone. Paint smeared on your car. Tools smashed. Who did this thing? And why? These were the questions I had.

I knew the invader's name. It was depression. But I didn't understand it.

For me, one of the most pleasurable parts of the books I have written has been the research. My friends don't understand this. They believe it is the act of turning the manuscript over to the publisher: "There, I'm done with it." Or having the book actually appear: "Here it is!" No, the love of this thing, the sheer wonder and enjoyment lies first of all in *learning*. In research you lose yourself in a world—lose yourself in order to find your way and try to recreate the way in the act of writing. There's the joy of the thing—this discovery and making.

But here I had entered enemy-held territory, and it was not a joy. Only a persistent determination to know the enemy, and Pat's plea for answers, drove me on.

This second thing about research. To do it properly you *must* lose yourself in that other world of the subject matter. But *this* world, mostly the care of Joel, demanded all my attention. Baby had to be fed, changed, washed, cuddled. If only he would keep my hours.

Why does he do his biggest mess, the kind that squirts up the back and slides down the legs, at 3:00 A.M.? Now that's not right. There is a cause and effect, I learned, between time and a baby's bowel movements. The earlier the hour, the huger the mess. This fact means, first of all, a good bath in the middle of the night. Probably for both of us since I never could change one of those cataclysmic dirty diapers on a squirming baby without getting it up to my elbows. This may be due to the fact that it happens at 3:00 A.M. You see the links in the chain of cause and effect. Never mind that parenting infants holds its own perverse logic.

So baby gets a bath. And then, of course, baby is lively and ready to play for a few hours. Who can resist that cooing, smiling, wiggling, clean little guy at 3:30? I can. I caught myself once planting the bottle nicely in Joel's left ear as I dozed off on the rocking chair. He thought it was great fun.

During our long ordeal a young couple in the neighborhood stopped by once with a fresh-baked peach pie.
At the time, I was feeding Joel some strange mixture of
plums and cereal, a wild purple mess that he loved to
let drool down his chin, examine with his chubby fingers
and rub through his blond hair. The young husband
looked at it all with disbelief. Then he murmured, with
a note of horror in his voice as the reality struck him,
"Do you have to change him, too?"

"Yeah," I said. "Once a day whether he needs it or
not."

Then there is this other problem. Despite the marvels
of disposable diapers, we have found that baby needs
several cloth diapers and a rubber pants at night. This
is because of the cause and effect I have just established.
Babies have their own logic. But wait. Sooner or later
those diapers—and the bedding, and all those dirty
sleepers, and towels—have to be washed. A fact I usually
discover around 5:00 A.M. when Joel has just fallen
asleep.

This washing of dirty diapers, I have discovered, is
not a task to be taken lightly. There is the odor to deal
with. I find that if I turn the radio up very loud the
diapers don't smell as bad. The louder the better. Duti-
fully, keeping beat to the blasting radio, I wring the
diapers, rinse, wash. I concoct my own secret ingredients
of Borax, Downy, etc. The recipe is magic. Whatever is
within reach on the laundry shelf, dump in a half cup.

How about a cup of coffee after that? After all, It's
6:30. Sure, but baby's awake again. Bright and cheery
and ready to start a day of play. And now the diapers
have to be folded, along with all those tiny T-shirts,
sleepers, sheets, play clothes. They have to be folded to
fit on the little shelf under the changing table. That way
I also discover that I left certain things in the dryer, or
have dropped a vital article on the washroom floor and

it never got washed. That's okay, it'll go in with the bedding. With some work, I can get four loads done by 8:00 A.M.

I give Joel his bottle and lay him on the floor to babble and bat his hands (look, he's clapping for me—take what you can get!) while I fold the clothes. I start musing about the course I taught last semester. How long ago that was! The course was "A Christian View of Tragedy, Comedy, and Tragicomedy." That latter category is when things get so bad you can only laugh your way out of them. Such is life, we reasoned then.

I recalled a discussion we had in that class on whether God has a sense of humor. We got started on it one day, and it led into several more days of discussion. We looked at those many passages in the Bible where Jesus shows his wit, his ironic responses to the Pharisees, his light-hearted responses to his disciples. What a wonderful sense of humor Jesus had.

While musing on this, and while folding the clothes, I glance at Joel babbling merrily on the floor. Somehow he has reached out with his little fist and grabbed the chewed up rawhide dog bone, which he is now contentedly gumming. Great! Would God chuckle at Joel gnawing the dog bone? The dog, I observed, eyed her bone sleepily and decided it was better to snooze. After a moment's hesitation, I decided to take the bone away.

The other kids are up. Their first question: "Have you heard from Mom?" Not yet.

Second question: "What's for breakfast?" Good question. I've got baby fruit—plums, peaches, applesauce—baby cereal. . . . "We'll make our own, Dad. Yours too." That's good. I love black eggs and burned toast. Really good if you use the jelly knife to dish the eggs. Mmmmm. Grape eggs.

Every morning at eleven I walk Joel around the block in the stroller. Each day he makes it a couple of yards further before he starts to roar. The Prince of Wails reigns on the morning air. We're making progress. The kids are clearing the breakfast table and are looking for clean clothes. They've been given chores: clip the lawn, make beds, vacuum the living room, throw out that dog bone! The same chores they always get. I take a walk at eleven. A good one too, because after he hits the stretch where he roars, Joel gets bored with the sound of his crying and falls sound asleep.

Grandma comes in two mornings a week to clean house and give me some free time. I take the girls shopping for groceries. How did Pat ever manage the shopping? My first grocery bill is $189. This for a week? For six people? I begin clipping coupons like an addict. The next time we shop I have $17 in coupon savings and feel like a lottery winner. I never play the lottery so this is as close as I can get. I'm thinking about these things— clean clothes, groceries, cleaning the house while I take Joel for his walk.

Those and other thoughts as one day slides into the next and they all seem alike. Over and over my thoughts turn to Pat, and a heaviness that dims even the brilliant summer morning lowers over me. Days are passing for her too:

Wednesday, June 19. The nurse awakened me at 7:00. I feel so hopeless. To be here seems like a bad dream. I saw Dr. Mulder after breakfast. He tells me I have a biological depression brought on by stress, the hormone imbalance after delivery, the genes I inherited, and the chemical imbalance in my brain. He prescribed Desipramine, 25 mg. three times a day. I might get a dry mouth, constipated and dizzy from it, and have some visual disturbance. I've cried all day. At supper time I'm allowed to leave to eat in the cafeteria. I've been on a flow sheet, meaning I get checked on every 15 minutes. . . . I read my Bible over and over to find God's promises. I believe them but can't feel them. . . .

Thursday, June 20. *I went to devotions again at 8:30. I need that to start the day. But again I keep crying. At 9:30 I met my therapist. He's very understanding. He too assured me I will get well. He said the medicine may take 7-10 days to work. I still feel hopeless—like I'll never get well. . . .*

Friday, June 21. *I awakened a lot last night. I keep rereading the Bible so that I can be reminded of God's loving care although I don't really feel it. Mornings are so hard. I had group therapy and that made me very upset. I couldn't concentrate and become involved in someone else's problems. At 1:00 p.m. I saw my therapist, Todd. I told him how sad and worried I still feel. He said that's because I'm so depressed. He said I'm the most depressed person on their team now. He told me that my crying doesn't offend anyone. I also had a consultation with a psychiatric intern. She was very nice. She made me count backwards from 100 by 7's. At 6:00 P.M. my dosage of Desipramine was increased to 50 mg. . . .*

While the June breeze flows through the cottonwoods in the park, the sound of children's laughter careens from the wading pool, the sweet thunk of a well-hit ball echoes from the tennis court, Joel drifts asleep.

It's a tricky move transferring sleeping Joel from the stroller outside to his crib inside. Silence must reign in the house. Someone strokes the dog to ward off any whines. The door slides open. I tiptoe the snoring bundle, so oblivious to our work, through the house to the crib. Success. Within thirty seconds I take the phone off the hook (the calls are incessant), stick it in the dishtowel drawer, and take myself to bed. I sleep like the baby—sound as a rock—for an hour. Somewhere in the house the kids have opened some cans and are brewing a lunch. I hear the clatter of dishes and the sounds of laughter and groans as I drift off. My last thought before falling asleep is this: I wonder how much an automatic dishwasher costs. . . .

I hate washing dishes. Diapers I can live with. A dirty house is manageable—a vacuum does wonders and who sees dust when you're busy? But dishes! I loathe them. They are vengeful in turn. They pile up there in the sink without a shred of conscience, mocking me by their teetering piles. They defy me. I mutter at them walking past.

"Go away, dishes. Beat it."

Still they stand there. And, as if to mock me further, they let food dry on them. They are wretched. And I would not do them at all, except for the fact that we have only eight baby bottles, and they *must* be washed. I can live with a baby chewing on the dog's bone, but not drinking out of used bottles. Unlike the dishes, I have a conscience. I toy with the idea of buying a whole case of bottles, but then I think of the grocery bill and the idea of washing 144 bottles at once.

Yes, I know the children could do them. Probably should. And sometimes they do. But they have other chores to do. And from the start I have insisted that they will carry out their normal lives as much as possible. Yes, dear children. Go to your friends. Play! I'll do these . . . dishes.

I'm doing them when my friend and colleague Ed stops by. He is too good a friend to give me a pitying look. He means to encourage me. I can't help it that I break down, but it's okay. He understands. And he is carrying a bag. "It's my famous bean soup recipe," he says, and hauls out of the bag enough beans and ham to feed us for a month, if the soup gets made. "If you don't have onions, I'll get some," he adds. "But everyone has onions." A quick inventory reveals that I have both onions and celery. And a big enough pot.

It's a good thought, and a good action—this thing of making bean soup. There's a certain satisfaction in slicing and dicing and boiling and immersing. Let it simmer, Ed had said. For how many hours? It wouldn't be ready by supper time anyway, but the pizza store delivers. After which I left the children with a babysitter and went to visit Pat.

Those visits were as important to me as to her. And it became a sacred time in the daily whirl. In his book *The Orphean Passages*, Walter Wangerin, Jr., defines faith as "a relationship with the living God—*enacted in this world*, this world of the furious swirl, in which all things flow."[8] These visits were an exercise in faith for us, enacted in the daily swirl of our lives. The grounds of the hospital were lovely, woods and fields stretching from the buildings, a huge pond in which ducks gabble noisily, flowers awash in the evening sun.

I stop by the head nurse's office and find out more of the information I had wanted to research. I pump her for answers, and she answers patiently, thoroughly, giving me the rudimentary data to pursue when I have the time.

When I have time. For now I want to get back home in time to put Joel to sleep for the night.

All the kids are playing in the park across the street with the babysitter when I return. The odor strikes me as soon as I walk in. What is that smell? Ah, refried beans. The bean soup has simmered to an orange gelatinous mass. I scoop out the pot, figuring I could freeze the remains for condensed bean soup, when I notice the loaf of banana bread a friend had left on the counter while I was out. It had a note attached: God will provide for you.

Yes, Lord. But who makes the bean soup?

Which is why I didn't lose myself in my research. It came in bits and pieces, when I found time. But I began to learn about this illness that had descended upon our household, insistent little chunks of information—the terms sounding foreign and obscure, threatening—that I wasn't able to put into order for some time.

I was beginning to understand this much. The admission report had already distinguished between external (*exogenous*) and internal (*endogenous*) factors contributing to depression, and had diagnosed Pat's illness as a biological depression in which there was a severe biochemical dysfunction. I learned that there are two broad categories for depression: unipolar and bipolar. Both of these categories are still attended by many unknowns, many ambiguities. Again this fact became clear. Since depression is so uniquely individual, it is very difficult to define neat categories. For example, some specialists call for two subdivisions of unipolar depression. The first would be a severe depressive episode, a one-time experience of the illness; the second would be repeated occurrences of severe depression. Both of these two are now called unipolar. But what do those two terms, *unipolar* and *bipolar*, mean?

Bipolar depression, sometimes called "manic" depression, is characterized by recurring mood shifts. The patient swings between "two poles," one a manic state of extreme giddiness called *euphoria* (meaning "good to bear"); the other a depressive state of extreme melancholy called *dysphoria* (meaning "hard to bear"). The terror of bipolar depression lies in the patient's utter lack of control over the mood shifts.

Bipolar depression requires its own special course of pharmaceutical treatment, based upon the belief that there is a biochemical imbalance in the brain, caused perhaps by genetic transmission (heredity factors) or abnormalities in the brain caused by other circumstances.

In the brain, tiny amounts of chemicals affect emotions, thoughts, and behavior as billions of neurons send messages across a network of gaps called synapses. In depression, something disrupts this marvelously intricate flow, this delicate electrical dance across microscopic spaces. One theory speculates that too little of the transmitter norepinephrine causes depression; too much of it causes manic depression. More recent theories hold that several transmitters are involved, serotonin and dopamine, for example.

It is helpful to think of this delicate relationship in simpler terms. Most of us know that spark plugs provide the electrical surge which fires the gasoline in the combustion chamber of a car engine. When the spark plug is clean, and functioning normally, the spark creates a small explosion which drives the piston. We take this for granted. Most of us never think of it. We turn the key in the ignition and drive off. All the while those spark plugs are doing their normal task.

They do that "normal" work, however, only if they are properly seated in place and properly adjusted. If they are adjusted wrong, for any number of reasons—the gap set too large, wear from overuse—the spark overheats and causes erratic performance. The car surges, backfires, slows down. The performance is analogous to bipolar depression.

If that same spark plug, furthermore, is fouled up, again for a variety of reasons—dirty fuel, extended use— the engine may begin to run sluggishly. It is difficult to start. Little energy is getting through to the combustion chamber. When it does start, the car lacks normal power. In this case the analogy is to unipolar depression.

While it may be helpful to think of this complex process in simpler terms of analogy, any analogy fails to capture all the activities involved. The brain is a tremendously mysterious organ, whose complex activities are still not fully understood by modern science. How we see its operations depends, in part, upon our perspective. In a special report in *Harper's Magazine* titled "The World of the Brain" we meet a thoroughly objective perspective. Staff editor Lawrence S. Burns offers this unflattering description:

> The human brain is a gelatinous three-pound lump of fat, connective tissue, spinal fluid, veins, and nerve cells— the last generating some twenty-five watts of total power. Without support from the cranium and the three membranes called the meninges, it would slump like a fallen soufflé. Though the brain is in constant contact with every living cell in the body, it can feel no pain itself. The brain is a greedy, thirsty, selfish vampire that guzzles a pint-and-a half of blood a minute. No matter what is happening in the body, the brain takes its nourishment first, because a minute without oxygen or glucose results in unconsciousness; eight minutes causes death. For some reason, the brain needs more blood when the body is asleep than when awake.[9]

Such a description, mechanical and factual, hardly touches the profound mysteries, the dazzling intricacy of activities, that one discovers by probing the *operations* of the brain. While analogies, then, help us understand the process of depression, they fail to capture the true complexity.

This complexity also affects the treatments for depression. In both of the analogies above, something breaks down in the energy transmitting process. But each requires a different treatment. So, too, the case with unipolar and bipolar depression. In Pat's case, her doctor prescribed the generic tricyclic Desipramine, which is marketed under the brand name of Norpramin or Pertofrone.

Another common generic tricyclic is Amitriptyline, marketed as Elavil, Endes, Etrafon, and Triavil.

Like all drugs, antidepressants have side effects which vary from patient to patient. Perhaps the most disconcerting side effect for Pat was the inability to exercise hard. Exercise has always been one of the hallmarks of our family activities. Our thrice weekly tennis matches on the courts across the street have been one of our favorite times together. People weren't used to seeing this small lady tear apart her husband with smashing volleys and hard baseline drives. In the evening we would often strike out on a two- or three-mile run. These were replaced now by sedate walks. Recent studies have confirmed that, beyond question, exercise is beneficial for depression and that it can even act as an antidepressant in our daily routine. Even if exercise has to be reduced to sedate walks, it can still occur.

In addition to these primary pharmaceutical treatments, the doctor is also likely to prescribe a tranquilizer to reduce anxiety. To help restore normal sleeping patterns, sleeping pills may also be prescribed.

I am well aware that discussion of such drugs makes many people nervous. Somehow, we feel we lose control to this foreign substance or that we are relying on "worldly" help too exclusively. Two items should be stressed here.

First, it is absolutely essential that the patient strictly follow the doctor's prescribed drug treatment. Antidepressants take some time, often several weeks, to reach therapeutic levels in the body's chemical system, and that therapeutic level must be maintained for a certain length of time to be fully effective. Sometimes, as a patient begins to feel a bit better, he or she will start missing the daily prescribed amount. The risk here is very serious; the delicate balance of chemicals, until it gets well within its normal pattern, can easily falter again.

The second important caution has to do with our socially-induced fear of drug dependency. All about us the media warn against drug abuse, until it begins to ring in our ears. To a certain extent this is a legitimate fear with any medicine. Knowledge of why the drugs are necessary and how they work is essential to the patient's well-being and full recovery. Still, many patients, particularly those experiencing the acute guilt and anxiety which depression often carries, will become fearful that they are overly reliant upon the drug.

Furthermore, in some Christian circles we find a tragic misunderstanding of this therapy, as indeed there is of the illness of depression itself. In his book *Depression: What It Is and What To Do About It*, Roger Barrett accurately assesses this misunderstanding and the unfortunate consequences of it. Barrett frankly states, "I especially get disturbed by those psycho-religious authors and speakers whose promises are totally out of proportion to the realities of depression and life. They suggest that if one will only get right with God, then depression will surely dissipate."[10] The approach, which he calls "spiritual boonswoggling," is "dishonest and deceitful. No one who has had long-term contact with depressed persons can maintain such simplistic approaches."[11]

Some popular religious magazines, and some books, are fairly riddled with this notion that depression can be overcome by reliance upon traditional Christian means such as prayer and Bible study. Articles with titles such as "How You Can Overcome Anxiety" abound today in response to our human needs in a complex society. The fault with many such articles is not that they're wrong. They are not. Prayer and Bible study are guards against anxiety. They are also critical to the course of treatment for depression. Rather, it is that such articles are insufficient and too inclusive. They are insufficient because some forms of anxiety or depression require medical intervention. They are too inclusive because there are as many different forms of anxiety and depression as there are individuals. This has to be recognized, and advice offered as a quick "cure-all" is often more damaging than helpful.

Such misunderstandings also attend pharmaceutical treatment of depression, which is a critical, necessary part of God's divine healing, a means of grace. Lillian Grissen, who has written candidly and forcefully about her own struggle with depression, strikes the better course. In an article in *The Banner*, of which she is managing editor, Grissen points out that "Depression expresses itself differently in different people," and adds, "I can speak only about what I experienced and fought for five years and suffered intermittently for much of my adult life. For me depression was

- being too tired to move my jaws up and down to chew lettuce,
- having recurring headaches that pounded like perpetually exploding bombs,
- crying hysterically at almost anything, even at the ring of the telephone or doorbell,
- trying to read and being unable to move my eyes past the first word,
- seeing and hearing my baby cry, but being too dull to give her a bottle,
- believing my children would be better off with a mother other than me,
- knowing that God wanted no part of me."[12]

Grissen credits her husband, her doctors, her God for her recovery, but also her pharmaceutical treatment. She clearly states the caution involved here: "I have been on mood-leveling and antidepressant medication for the past seven years. It still hurts to hear Christian leaders say too easily, 'People think if they are down, they can take a little pill to cure everything.' They make it sound as though doctors should not prescribe pills for depression. That's a mistake. One of the blessings of modern research and technology is the medicine that helps depressed people function."[13]

Her comments are well-put. If the first lesson Pat and I had to learn was to seek help, this second lesson was equally urgent: to accept and understand the process of that help.

4 Postpartum Depression: The Medical Phenomenon

P at's illness received the medical diagnosis of "severe, major biological depression." While this defines it rather neatly as a medical phenomenon, it still left questions in our minds. How did the medical phenomenon come about? Clearly, her illness seemed to be related to certain triggering events—most notably her late pregnancy. While doctors repeatedly assured us that the pregnancy was not the cause of the depression, it was impossible to evade this hard question: Would the depression have occurred apart from the pregnancy? The easy response is this: We don't know. It didn't happen that way. The harder issue, however, is this: What do we make of the way it did happen?

First of all, we must understand some of the reasons for the doctors' assurances that the *baby* was not the cause. A depressed person typically feels enormous guilt because of the illness. If one of the symptoms of the illness is a loss of self-worth, characteristically this manifests itself in the feeling that I have failed in my obligations.

Therefore, I am unworthy. Therefore, I am guilty. A new mother feels her greatest responsibility to the child she has nurtured for nine months of pregnancy and now in life. A bond is formed that simply goes beyond the comprehension of those who have not shared the experience. Thus the acute focus of the mother's guilt lies in her sense of having failed the infant who is chiefly dependent upon her. It is essential that this guilt be alleviated. It is one of the most damaging symptoms of the depression: I have failed those who need me most.

The careful and insistent reassurances of Pat's doctors from the start did much to alleviate her sense of guilt and failure. Nonetheless, her journals reveal how often her thoughts turn to the family, and her sense of discouragement in not being able to fulfill her customary role.

July 8. Tim visited with Joel, Tammy, and Betsy. Joel then went home with Bob and Ruth [brother and sister-in-law]. It was a good visit. I fed Joel and he was real sweet. I felt very lonely and discouraged after they left.

July 9. This morning I awakened feeling very homesick and also very lonely for the children and Tim. I prayed for each of them individually and had many tears of loneliness.

July 11. When I came out of class Mom was here and so was Tim with Joel. I still worry about the stress at home being too much for him. I plead with God to keep him and the children secure and safe and free from the depression.

At other times Pat's feelings of failure became more pronounced. It is not difficult to see how this pattern of worry about the family, and loneliness in being apart from the family, can be accompanied by feelings of guilt.

This second pattern often occurs in postpartum depression. Although not the case in Pat's depression, it is not unusual for the parents or siblings to feel some anger at the baby as a *cause*. This is an understandable human response. Something bad has happened; we try to locate the agent to turn our anger against it. Modern society programs us for this response. In the incidence of a crime, we hope to find the criminal and prosecute him in the courts. The punishment enacts the anger we justly feel against the wrong of the criminal. Human emotions are like that. And the mother is not immune against that human emotion. The thinking might arise like this: Had I not had this baby, I wouldn't be ill. Therefore, anger is directed at the child, often subconsciously or without fully realizing it.

As we understand the human emotions involved, we can also understand the need to guard against them. In our particular situation this problem did not arise. Curiously, it arose in some others who sought to counsel us or who wanted to visit a problem on us that we did not have. More than once the question was raised whether the baby was the cause, or whether we resented the baby. At first, our response was that we had never thought of it. But as the questions persisted, we realized that we had to think of it.

Doing so, we realized the wisdom of the doctors' advice and the tragic effects of such emotions turned upon the child. Resentment directed at this infant could scar the him for life. These are emotions that must be confronted and understood.

Just as there are two ways to write novels—realism (this could have happened) and fantasy (could this happen?)—there are two ways to address this issue. Although we received assuring responses from doctors, although we knew how much we loved this baby, it would be unrealistic to say the question of cause and effect *never* arose. One of the children, for example, might ask in all innocence: "Did our baby cause this?"

The answer really, truly, was no. Yet we can't live in fantasies when dealing with depression either. Let me emphasize the fact that it is difficult to pinpoint exact causes for depression. The elements contributing to it are so varied and wide in scope that none deserve the full blame. But combined in just the right mix and intensity, hormonal imbalance, hereditary disposition, personality, social pressures to perform, and poor self-image can result in clinical depression.

In my desire to understand all possible contributing factors to Pat's illness, I scoured texts, journals, and papers on the postpartum period. Clearly discernible is a link between the biological process of pregnancy and delivery and the biological process of depression. Although convincing studies have not thoroughly corroborated it, neither have they dispelled the fact that acute biological changes occur in a woman during delivery and birth that wrench the body's gears unbelievably.

It has often been stated that the three pressure points for women in regard to depression are premenstrual syndrome, menopause, and the postpartum period. Although the first two undoubtedly evoke feelings of the "blues" in women and do affect her biological chemistry, scientific studies have failed to draw a conclusive link between them and clinical depression. In an article published in *Women and Psychotherapy: An Assessment of Research and Practice*, the authors point out that the failure to establish a connective link may be due more to faulty research processes than the existence of a link itself. "Research in this area," they point out, "has been relatively sparse and uneven. It has been criticized methodologically for sloppiness of definitions, sampling, and approach. . . . Those studies which are considered more reliable show that psychosomatic and psychological complaints were not reported more frequently by so-called 'menopausal' than by younger women."[14] They conclude that "Menopause can be considered as one of the important experiences for women but one that is best understood in the context of their lives, their particular experiences and adaptive responses, and their sociocultural environment with its value systems."[15]

On the other hand, it is difficult to dispute the increased incidence of depression first among women and second among women during times of greatest hormonal change. Considering this, Alan Frazer and Andrew Winokur in their *Biological Bases of Psychiatric Disorders* assert that

> There is considerable evidence that factors associated with aspects of sex hormone functions may be of importance in our understanding of the development of depression. Thus, depression is more common in females than in males, especially among unipolar depressives (this may be due to genetic rather than to hormonal factors): depression is more likely to occur at times of endocrine change premenstrually, *postpartum*, at the menopause, or in association with oral contraceptive administration.[16]

The lack of firm scientific evidence drives us to the conclusion that "it might be." This is not a comfortable conclusion from a scientific point of view. Increasingly, however, scientific studies are pointing toward dramatic links among hormonal functions, chemical functions in the brain, and psychological states.

The question becomes then whether the postpartum experience has a relation to clinical depression, that is, a syndrome that includes a number of specific symptoms that are severe, persistent, and disabling—symptoms such as those set forth in chapter two. To answer this question adequately, however, we must consider a complex of several factors coming to bear upon the birth experience.

The woman who has just given birth, whom we will call the "new mother" regardless of how many children she has, lives in an unsettled and unsettling world. For nine months she has been acutely aware, inescapably aware, of the changes in her body. She has seen doctors, prepared for delivery, and has seen herself differently than before. Suddenly, after birth, the only doctor she is likely to see, apart from a follow-up visit to the obstetrician, is the pediatrician. The baby's needs come first. The preparations for delivery have vanished in the hard work of labor and the hard work of caring for the infant. Now she sees herself differently, sometimes even a bit like one caught in a trap of endless demands upon her time and energy. The baby now reigns supreme. Carol Dix, author of *The New Mother Syndrome: Coping with Postpartum Stress and Depression*, puts it like this:

> We promote the idea that all the care and information about pregnancy and birth should be packed into the nine months *before* the baby arrives, and that no information or support should be given to mothers (or fathers) once the baby has arrived, other than tips on diapering, burping, and promoting baby's sleep.[17]

The focus is changed from the mother as the woman carrying a baby to the mother struggling to keep up with the baby's ever-changing needs. A kind of psychological displacement results. In some cases it seems to the mother that she has become a kind of function rather than a person.

This is often aggravated by a second set of circumstances. As never before, our culture insistently urges women to *be* certain things. Two forces actually come to bear here. On the one hand, we see a heightened awareness of the worth of womanhood, an idea nurtured by sound, reflective Christians who believe that women too have been gifted by God and deserve the opportunity to fulfill these gifts. No matter what the woman does, such thinking goes, she is an image-bearer of God, she is gifted by God, she is called by God to fulfill her gifts. For a new mother, however, it may be difficult for her to see herself as anything but a functionary, subject to the whims and demands of the child, rather than as a person fulfilling her individual gifts. One might very sensibly respond that motherhood in itself is both a gift and a calling, a means for glorifying God. While our concern here is not with the validity of these views that are the focus of attention today, our concern is very much with the effect that the tug and pull of these ideas can have on a new mother. She might very well be led to believe she is less than worthy in her role as mother. Right or wrong, it remains an unavoidable consideration in the context of our modern Christian society.

On the other hand, the more strident voices of some contemporary feminists tell women that motherhood in and of itself is a thing of secondary importance. The National Organization of Women, for example, insists that abortion is the fundamental right of a woman to ensure her independence to fulfill herself. Although they argue that motherhood is something the woman should be free to choose, the implications of their radical stance on abortion suggest that the child doesn't count, that as long as a woman is "in bondage" to childbearing she will never be free to be fully female. The insidiousness of this thinking is also inescapable. Again, the mother's self-image is called into question. Again, the question arises—Am I a captive of motherhood? Am I no longer a woman, but merely a function?

We see, then, that first of all there is the danger of a lack of an immediate support network for the new mother, and secondly that contemporary society implies that mothering is a second-class occupation, thereby calling the new mother's self-image into question. When we have a lack of support and questions about self-worth working together, we begin to see the potential for danger. A third factor, one of great significance for Pat and me, enters in. We must consider the tremendous physical effort that occurs during childbirth and the physiological changes that occur internally. From head to toe the mother's body during birth is a network of muscles working harder together than they are likely to do at any other time of her life. Not only are her muscles contracting, squeezing, bulging, and working for every ounce of strength, but her body is twisting its very shape, with organs, intestines, and muscles literally moving from one position to another. And at this very moment when the muscles are asking for every drop of energizing blood they can get, her body is losing its blood-carried energy. A mother in labor is running a hard marathon every hour that ticks by. No wonder she is exhausted.

There was a day, of course, when men didn't know this. Giving birth was a woman's business and the menfolk would find some convenient excuse to visit elsewhere or to walk nervously in some hallway outside the reach of the delivery room's noises. One effect of the explosion in childbirth classes in the last decade has been to involve the father more directly and intimately in the birth process. More than one father has emerged astonished not just at the beauty of the birth but also at the tremendously hard work of the birth.

Along with the massive physical effort, the body's glands are racing into overdrive, trying to refuel the depleting resources to guide the course of this marathon. But at that very moment, the maternal hormones are also changing course. For nine months the mother's body has been working steadily, systematically to nest that precious infant. Carol Dix states that "By the time a woman goes into labor, the levels of her estrogen and progesterone, for example, are fifty times higher than before a pregnancy." She adds, "The most acute hormonal change happens on the first day after delivery, when progesterone and estrogen levels plunge dramatically. Within twenty-four to thirty-six hours after childbirth the estrogen and progesterone fall from these high levels to levels that are below prepregnancy levels."[18]

Think of the wildest roller coaster ride in any park that you can name; then place it inside the mother in labor. This is the physiological turmoil of her body.

Such physical factors as these may contribute to the temporary disturbance of mood that we call the "blues" in many new mothers, particularly during the period of three to fifteen days following delivery. In fact, the so-called "three day blues" or "the weepies" are so common that some women feel odd if they don't have them. This is a short-lived syndrome afflicting perhaps up to 80 percent of mothers with some symptoms of anxiety, restlessness, and sadness for varying periods of time, sometimes several hours, sometimes several days. It can be triggered by a number of events. Dix suggests that "It can be set off by feelings of rejection; the doctor not showing proper attention, one's husband coming late to visit at the hospital, a nurse or orderly being offhand or rude; by good news, such as another birth in the family; or by a sense of inadequacy, if the milk doesn't come in properly or we have problems with breastfeeding."[19] The link between the tremendous bodily upheavals and the mood is evident.

But consider that in some cases that roller coaster ride inside the mother, the rocketing pitch of neurotransmitters, glands, and organs racing through their intricate network begin to twist awry. Such a situation may instigate the clinical depression that appears usually some fifteen to forty days after delivery.

The biological tie between postpartum depression and the bodily functions lies in the endocrine or hormonal system of the body. Its function may be understood by the Greek root of the word *hormone*: "to set in motion." The hormones are messengers or stimulators that are secreted by the body's major glands—thyroid, parathyroid, adrenals, pancreas, and gonads—and that travel through the bloodstream to the organs they regulate. Such glands, for example, send the hormones that start the miraculous changes in the uterus to nest the baby. And when the baby is born, these glands send the prolactin for breast-feeding.

But what tells the glands what to do? The brain has its own set of hormones emerging from the pituitary and regulated by the hypothalamus. These neurohormones, so called because the neurons are the transmitters of the hormones—dopamine, serotonin, and norepinephrine being the most common—travel through the network of passages that is the brain, sending out signals across tiny synapses. These signal the body's endocrine system to provide the estrogen, the progesterone, and the prolactin for the organs. Thus we see a link between brain and body. Carol Dix points out that

> After childbirth, we experience major endocrine changes: the rapid drop in estrogen and progesterone, the two main hormones of pregnancy, comes within hours of delivery. There are also falls in thyroid levels (to a point lower than the prepregnant state), and a decrease in pituitary function. At the same time, we undergo massive blood loss and drop in body fluids; prolactin is increased for breast-feeding; there is sleep disturbance; and we experience other, more technical, changes, such as altered levels of adrenal steroids, free and binding corticosteroids, and gonadotrophins.[20]

This massive change in bodily hormones is accompanied by commensurate changes in the neurohormone system. As the bodily glands decrease their hormones, the hypothalamus similarly seems to decrease the neurohormones, thus creating the sluggishness between the neurons that indicates depression.

But the hypothalamus and these tiny neurons do a great deal more. They also regulate activities such as sleep and appetite. The hypothalamus's job, in a way, is as a kind of regulator among many stimuli and messages. It has to balance the body's chemical network.

With the tremendous upheavals in the mother's hormonal balance following delivery, internal stress is thrown upon that regulator. At the very moment when the body pleads for rest and sleep, the mother's sleep is broken into ragged little nuggets.

Seen in this light, the link between body and brain appears so strong that the endocrine system is often referred to by the larger term *psychoendocrine* system. It is a system only recently emerging to the light of understanding. A *Newsweek* cover story on hormones quotes from Dr. C. Wayne Bardin, a biomedical researcher: "It [the process of thought] involves the interaction of hundreds, maybe thousands, of cells, yet we're still trying to understand at the level of simple cell."[21] The research in hormone function is similarly at an infant stage in ascertaining the great complexity of activities. The same article indicates that "as recently as 1970, only about 20 human hormones had been identified; now researchers think there may be as many as 200."[22] About forty-five such hormones have been identified in the brain, many of which perform different tasks elsewhere in the body, thus affirming the psychoendocrine relationship. The conclusion we draw, however, is that the physiological changes of the postpartum period can contribute to depression. Having drawn that conclusion, what significant points emerge? There are several. First, careful attention should be given in prenatal classes and in the popular Lamaze classes to the physiology of the mother during and after labor. Mothers need more thoughtful and thorough preparation for the *entire process* of childbirth. As parents of four children, we have attended many such prenatal classes. They all seem to end at the same point: a plastic doll slides through a model. And the class is done. We study the growth of the baby week by week until delivery, then stop our study. Sometimes mention is made of breast-feeding or postnatal care of the infant. But the mother? No, the class ends with the birth of the baby. But a new kind of life just begins there for the mother, and this life—physiological, psychological, and social—must be addressed in such classes.

Childbirth is a glorious event, bringing into life an image bearer of God. Someone once remarked that children are the only treasure that we can take to heaven with us. Childbirth, then, opens a door on eternity. But a kind of false glorification also attends childbirth.

Already in the hospital and shortly after the return home, the new parents will receive advertising brochures and magazines for baby products. Like nearly all aspects of the advertising world, these items artificially glamorize childbearing and rearing. Each parent wears a 1000-watt smile that lights up a baby who seems never, ever to cry, wet, spit up, or be just plain ornery. Where do they get these idyllic children? Now, granted, we don't want the people who hawk baby goods in advertisements wearing sullen, dour frowns. We want childbearing to be happy. But imagine the mother who feels like a steam roller has just driven over her body, and dragged her a couple of blocks in addition, seeing those happy, happy faces. Somehow her reality doesn't match up to the ideal. What's wrong with me? she wonders.

This popular glorification in the baby books and advertising brochures tends to deny the realities of the delivery and post-delivery periods. Having built this bubble of glorious anticipation, the hard crushing blow of depression can easily cause intolerable guilt in the mother. "I should be so happy. Everyone else is. Why do I feel like this? It must be my fault." So the reasoning goes.

The plain truth is that to be forewarned is to be prepared. Depression creeps upon a person so insidiously that she often doesn't know it is an overwhelming problem until it overwhelms. That's too late. Prenatal classes must contain information on the delivery and post-delivery biological changes in the mother. Indeed, it is not always as pleasant as the glamorized anticipation of birth, but it is realistic and can make the days after birth far more pleasant simply by supplying an understanding of what is happening internally.

Second, we observe that there is entirely too much pressure to conform to some lofty ideal of "motherhood." Modern society leaves far too little room for individual needs and for failure. Let us provide a personal example. Because our first baby was adopted, he was bottle fed. When Betsy was born just eleven months later, at a time when Dad was in the last year of Ph.D. studies and Mom was working part-time as a nurse, things were just too hectic and inconvenient for breast-feeding. And when Tammy was born, she developed a severe jaundice which doctors at that time thought was present because of a reaction to breast milk. Finally, with Joel, Pat had the chance to breast-feed.

It seemed, however, that she was doing it twenty-four hours a day. We recognized the many good points about breast-feeding. How could we not, with advocates for it all around us? But devoting that huge amount of time to breast-feeding, with the needs of a busy family, began to exact a toll. When Pat suggested to a friend that she was thinking of switching over to bottle-feeding, this friend lectured her at some length on all the benefits of breast-feeding, leaving no room for doubt that failure to do so would be just that—failure. "It helps bonding with the infant," the friend said. But what happens when you're so bound you're becoming unglued? "It's so good for the baby," the friend insisted. But what about the good of the mother?

We have to be realistic about the fact that each of us is unique, with individual needs and demands. Others tend to push their successes or even some current fad upon us. Sometimes we have to be willing to find our own best way and feel good about it because it is best for us, regardless of what others say.

Third, we observe that medical doctors should include as part of the post-delivery and follow-up examinations of the mother an inventory of her psychological well-being three to four weeks following delivery. Obstetricians are busy people and, to be sure, their major job is accomplished with the birth of the baby. But after that birth the mother is often at a loss where to turn with her special needs. The routine six-week checkup is likely to be little more than that, a hurried checkup, especially in light of the "postpartum pinks," the good mood or euphoria during delivery. A study reported in the *American Journal of Psychiatry* found that "even mothers who were dysphoric during pregnancy and later became blue or depressed again reported relative well-being, joy, and surprise immediately after delivery."[23] It is important to recognize the phenomenon, for it helps explain why a doctor's initial observation of a woman shortly after birth may lead the doctor to believe the woman is in completely good spirits. It also explains why, in these researchers' view, "all our subjects were discharged from the hospital without special counseling or psychiatric referral." They conclude that "even women who look well after delivery can be at risk for both mild and severe psychiatric disturbance in the weeks and months that follow."[24]

In the same study reported in the *American Journal of Psychiatry*, a team of medical researchers attempted to find "valid predictors" of postpartum mood disorder. In the fashion typical of studies in this journal, the methodology of the study was carefully structured. A group of twenty pregnant women monitored their emotions for indications of depression at twenty-six and thirty-six weeks of pregnancy, and again at two days and six weeks postpartum. The monitoring was completed by a clinical interview.

Observing the increased vulnerability to depression during the postpartum period, the researchers summarize some of the current theories accounting for this. One large area of such theorizing has to do with stress factors. While affirming that "a close confiding relationship with another person, usually a spouse, can protect against depression in the face of social stress," research indicates that other stressful events, other than the birth of the child, "were associated with mild postpartum depression."[25] By recognizing during the pregnancy certain stressful factors—including life events, relations with other people, attitudes toward the pregnancy itself—the potential for postpartum mood disorders can be predicted with a fairly high degree of accuracy.

The value of such studies lies in their enforcing the need for close scrutiny of pregnant women's moods both during and following pregnancy and delivery. This study indicated that 60 percent of women experience postpartum "blues," a figure comparing favorably with figures of 50 percent and 66.7 percent of two earlier, 1968, studies. The authors conclude that "our findings confirm that postpartum women should be considered a risk and screened for emotional distress."[26]

We do not intend to lay blame at the feet of the medical

profession. Nonetheless, one recognizes a large gap between the work of the obstetrician and the work of the psychiatrist. Somewhere there should be a more specific link between them. Of the dozens of books researched for this chapter, including standard textbooks used to train medical personnel, the scarcity of discussion on depressive disorders following birth was astonishing. One textbook, which provides an entire lengthy chapter on abortion procedures, offered no more than two sentences on the possibility of postpartum depressive disorders. One sentence encouraged the physician to inquire about the mother's feelings and home life. The second encouraged the physician to make a referral if something seemed amiss. The books on prenatal health care were no better; they routinely ended with the delivery. Such information as the mother receives on postpartum disorders is likely to be received from family, friends, or hard experience, rather than from an authoritative, helping resource. While the mother experiencing difficulty needs support from family and friends, she also needs prompt and decisive medical attention.

The link we are looking for may be as simple as the systematic administration of screening questionnaires to determine potential for depression in pregnant women. Several such tools exist (see Braverman and Roux, "Screening for the Patient at Risk for Postpartum Depression" *Obstetrics and Gynecology*, 52 (1978): 731, 736. Tools for mood assessment do exist and ought to be employed as part of the total health care of the pregnant woman.

One is gratified, however, that despite such cautions there is a growing concern among obstetricians and gynecologists for the woman's unique psychological needs. The total picture, while not yet ideal, is becoming more optimistic. As the studies that we do have continue to supply evidence, one finds the medical profession responding more aggressively to these needs. This was the case with Pat's doctor and his quick and decisive action to gain her admittance for hospitalization.

Finally, we observe the need for postnatal support networks. These are being formed in many communities. At some levels they may be informal arrangements of friends or church members. For example, a group of women of a church might see it as their Christian service to plan visits with new mothers in order to become aware of any problems. At other levels these support networks are extensions of prenatal classes. Our suggestion is that all prenatal classes at the very least schedule one or more post-birth classes to deal with the realities of mothering the newborn.

We see, then, a complex relationship of hormonal activities coming to bear upon the psychological condition of the postpartum period. At the very least, this ought to make us acutely sensitive to the physical and psychological needs of the mother. In addition, such understanding casts greater light upon the phenomenon of postpartum depression. We recognize this activity and this need for several reasons: to avoid casting blame upon the infant as "cause," to alleviate the guilt incurred by postpartum depression in the mother, and to understand better the biochemical nature of the illness. Furthermore, such a recognition leads us to a consideration of a more realistic picture of the total birth process, of the individual needs of each mother, of the need for greater medical awareness of postpartum depression, and of the need for a support network for the new mother.

5   The Grip of the Undertow: Walking by Faith, Not by Sight

"All perfection hath some imperfection joined to it in this life, and all our power of sight is not without some darkness." So wrote Thomas À Kempis in *The Imitation of Christ*.

All perfection has some imperfection joined to it. How can we understand this? The world itself was created good, made by God, who is perfection itself. But imperfection is now joined to it. We live in a world which humanity has tipped from its pinnacle of perfection.

The perfection has not been destroyed or rubbed out. No power can do that to the supreme power of God, else he would not be God. That is why David can say, "This God—his way is perfect; the promise of the LORD proves true; he is a shield for all those who take refuge in him" (Psalm 18:30). Goodness still beats through this world, else David would not have been able to sing, "The heavens are telling the glory of God; and the firmament proclaims his handiwork" (Psalm 19:1). The perfection of God shines through the darkness; the darkness of imperfection has not overcome it. *If God is the perfect light of the world, imperfection has placed a kind of veil upon how we see that light.* The light still shines, despite the imperfections of our seeing.

Because of imperfection—and how we wish it were not so!—there are times when the light seems dim and the imperfection all too large. We wish it were an even line, that the light of perfection would shine with consistent clarity so that we could clearly place the darkness of imperfection into closets and shut the door upon it. There! Stay there! So we wish to tame the darkness, to domesticate it. If we recognize the haze of perfection and imperfection, we still fail to understand the surge of darkness like incoming and receding waves.

We know that it has been so since that first moment when humanity, through the tempter Satan, drew the veil of haze over God's brilliant perfection. We know this to be so. We can't understand it. That is the curse of imperfection and darkness. But we are not alone in this.

Consider Job.

Cursing the day of his birth, Job cried, "Let gloom and deep darkness claim it . . . let the blackness of the day terrify it" (3:5). And why did Job say this? Because the light of perfection seemed to have receded from his life. He recognized it, but he could not understand it. Thus he cries: "Behold, I go forward, but he is not there; and backward, but I cannot perceive him; on the left hand I seek him, but I cannot behold him. I turn to the right hand, but I cannot see him" (23:8-9). Job felt forsaken, overwhelmed in a sea of dark imperfection, lost from the light of God.

Consider David.

He was in the desert, lonely and wandering. This was the dry place of the spirit, where the terror of darkness overwhelmed him, and he lifted his lonely cry: "I cry aloud to God, aloud to God, that he may hear me. In

the day of my trouble I seek the Lord; in the night my
hand is stretched out without wearying, my soul refuses
to be comforted" (Psalm 77:1-2). Although he affirmed
the perfect light, David knew well the dark imperfection
of life. This was not one big wave that crashed over him
from which he could arise, momentarily bruised but
rejoicing in the sunlight; rather, the breakers roll, bearing
him down and down to that point where he cries, "Why
dost thou stand afar off, O LORD? Why dost thou hide
thyself in times of trouble?" (Psalm 10:1). David felt forsaken, as if, at the time when he needed God most, God
was hidden behind the haze of dark imperfection.

Consider Isaiah.

He seemed like the last of the righteous in a land that
had forsaken God. Was his the only voice testifying to
the light? Why did no one listen? When he looked about
him, he saw the tide of blackness—the idol worship, the
astrology, the blasphemous sacrifices—and decreed that
"they will look to the earth, but behold, distress and
darkness, the gloom of anguish; and they will be thrust
into thick darkness" (Isaiah 8:22). Evil lay like a malevolent pall upon the land. And Isaiah's voice seemed like
a whisper against the roar of confusion.

Consider Jesus.

Here stands the true light himself, the light of the
world, the Bright Morning Star, the very son of God.
And how does he stand? In the form of humanity; the
very same who marred God's perfection, who cast the
darkness over that light. To restore the light, Jesus underwent the full anguish of darkness. None could know
this more profoundly: to experience, as the perfect light,
the perfect darkness; to know separation from God so
thoroughly; to plumb the deepest sea of darkness so
that he could build a bridge out of it for us. He could
not do that without enduring the most terrifying separation from God into darkness. And Jesus cries, with the

echo of Job, of David, of Isaiah, of all those afflicted by darkness through the centuries—thus he cries—"My God. My God. Why hast thou forsaken me?"

To be cut off from God. But more than this: from his Father God. To be forsaken. But more than this: to be plunged to the heart of dark imperfection.

In an article titled "A Love So Fierce," theologian Cornelius Plantinga, Jr., convincingly ties our human suffering to the suffering of Jesus. Sometimes, Plantinga argues, we fail to comprehend the urgent relevance of the cross to our own suffering:

> I know that the cross can be decorated in popular piety and domesticated and trivialized. Still, in suffering we need to turn toward the cross. For in the passion and death of Jesus we see the same blend of inevitability and outrage that we see in our own; indeed, we see the very mold, the very prototype of it.[27]

At such a moment, Plantinga points out, Jesus' cry joins the cries of countless others who are pounded in the sea of suffering. Here is the prophetic fulfillment not only of Isaiah's words but also of the Christian plea: "Thus Jesus Christ bears our griefs and carries our sorrows. He was sharing the lot of all who cry half-devout, half-profane 'O my God!' when they are stabbed with the knowledge of death. He then shares the lot of those who nonetheless entrust themselves into the hands of a God who, as C.S. Lewis once said, 'knows how to do such fearful things with those hands.'"

What is the meaning of Jesus' suffering, of the cross, then? Is it only the heartbroken cry? No. Plantinga observes that the cross is ultimately his sign of fierce love: "The cross of Jesus Christ—this ugly thing stuck up like a scarecrow in the center of our religion—tells us of a love so fierce, so determined . . . that its bearer is willing to be humiliated and tortured and bewildered and, for a time, to be dead."[28]

A friend of ours has a plaque on her living room wall. It's probably a common saying on that plaque, yet each time I see it the words strike me afresh: "I asked Jesus 'how much do you love me?' Jesus said 'this much.' And he stretched out his arms, and he died." This love he has given to us who grope in the dark imperfection, and he gives it from the dark imperfection itself—a ray of light.

Yet we cry out, why hast thou forsaken me? We cannot understand why it happens to *us*: we want to see the light but the waves of darkness pound over us.

But does the darkness ever *overpower* the light?

The story of Job is incomplete until we read the song of Job, "I know that thou canst do all things, and that no purpose of thine can be thwarted" (Job 42:2).

The lament of David is incomplete until we read his hymn of joy. "Weeping," writes David, "may tarry for the night, but joy comes with the morning" (Psalm 30:5). The light will crash through the waves. Only hold on. God will not forsake you to the waves.

And the lonely cry of Isaiah, drowned out in the roar of confusion, is incomplete until we hear him proclaim God's promise that "They who wait for the LORD shall renew their strength, they shall mount up with wings like eagles, they shall run and not be weary, they shall walk and not faint" (Isaiah 40:31).

And Jesus? Forsaken? Bereft of the light and plunged into darkness? The Bright Morning Star seized from the heavens and plunged into the sea of human despair? The devil could not hold him. The darkness can never contain the light, for the darkness, by its very definition, is simply a deprivation of light. *It is dependent upon light for its very meaning*. Without light, we would not know what the darkness is. And how can the darkness, then, hold the light of the world? A shattered grave, blasted apart by the light of all ages, is the testimony. In the gutted wreck of that grave lies the foot of the bridge out of all darkness.

That is where our hearts turn—to the light of the Bright Morning Star. But this we also know, and it is grim: that we walk through this life on a way plunged between perfect light and dark imperfection. It was this point—where the breakers suck and pull on the mind as if it were a worthless toy—that our lives had now reached in the battle with depression.

Each expectation of some improvement, some success in Pat's medical condition during those early weeks of hospitalization, was met by setback. As a few steps were made toward the shore, another wave pulled her under. At the time, we were only aware of a baffling uncertainty. Looking back at the journal entries, we can see the ebb and flow.

Sunday, June 23. When I awaken, I have a sick feeling as I remember that I am here. Sometimes it still seems like a bad dream. Sally, my special nurse, talked with me. I told her how much I worry about my family. I attended chapel but found it very hard to concentrate. The message seemed meaningless to me. I'm feeling less depressed today. Like I'm able to smile again. Rand and Marijo [a brother and sister-in-law] came. I cried when they left. Tim and the three older children came for supper with me. I really enjoyed their visit. Nancy Vanden Berg is at home with Joel. How I thank God for friends.

Monday, June 24. Today I don't feel as depressed when I awaken. I am very lonesome for the children, so I called home. My medicine is increased again to 150 mg. each day. I went to psychodrama this afternoon and found that was something I couldn't relate to. I saw Todd [a therapist] this afternoon. He put me on unaccompanied status at my request. I may go out for dinner with Tim on Wednesday and lunch with Mom on

Thursday. He thought that might be too soon, but I can try it. . . . Dear God, please protect and keep my precious family. I miss them so much.

Tuesday, June 25. *One week done. I slept quite well without a sleeping pill. I feel like things look much brighter today. The day was very, very busy. The group interaction class consisted of two questions to ask each person in the group. The assertion class is more enjoyable. . . .*

Our attention is caught by the note: "One week done." We still thought, at this time, that the hospitalization would last about two weeks, perhaps three at the very most.

Hospitals everywhere have a kind of strange, other-worldly quality for me—and "blessed is the man who enters not therein" is my general attitude toward them. Perhaps my distrust resides in an unpleasant experience while confined to a military hospital for seven days when I was in the Army. I felt that, like Dante, I had entered the seventh circle of Hades. This hospital, however, immediately struck me differently. The sense of threat was blessedly absent, replaced by a strange feeling of a medical family. Moreover, I felt a part of it—not an untutored outsider—from the start.

Curiously enough, it reminded me of an experience a half dozen years earlier when our family went with some young adults from our church on a mission work project to the delta region of Mississippi. We came as "foreigners," to be sure, armed with shovels to dig new plumbing lines, hammers and saws to repair dwellings in one of the most depressed areas of North America. For a week we waded in mud and sawdust. Our reward came at the Shiloh Missionary Baptist Church on Sunday morning, just before our departure.

It had been a hard nine days of work, leaving indelible portraits in our minds. These remain. Jeffrey and Betsy knee-deep in a pit of mud bailing water and clay with empty paint cans. The water table here is eighteen inches. The pit for the new septic tank has to be six feet deep.

Mud in their hair, mud on their arms, mud crawling along their legs. The water is cold. But they stay willingly at the task. Someone calls at Betsy, seeing her disheveled blond curls, "Hey, Little Bo Peep!"

Finally the septic tank is in. The plumbing is connected to a new bathroom in a house that has never known plumbing. There are only four leaks at first, quickly repaired. Mr. Willis is ushered in to inspect his new bathroom. From behind the closed door we hear him weeping.

Mrs. Hunter has invited us in to see her patchwork quilts. She does one each winter, sitting on the edge of her bed before the small coal heater. She has twenty quilts to display.

When her house is finished—painted, windows caulked against the winter storms, new screens, new boards where the roof eaves rotted off—she is invited outdoors for a picture before her new house.

She combs her hair. Leaves her cane behind. Stands in front of her porch. Stares long and lonely at the setting sun while someone snaps her picture. She will not look into the camera. She holds someone's arm to walk around the house.

Mrs. Reuben Joiner shows us her prize chickens, all forty-two of them. "They's like my children," she says. "An old person's got to have children around." She invites us in. Her kitchen floor, which had rotted through to gaping holes, has been replaced. The house smells of propane escaping from the stove. A sliced potato boils on the stove. Someone hustles for a tool kit to repair the propane leak. Her husband, the Reverend Mr. Reuben Joiner, sits in the back yard stroking a chicken that rests in his lap. Tammy, wearing my windbreaker that falls below her knees, hands them the warm dinner Pat has prepared.

At the local store an old man taps his cane on the floor, sits on a barrel by the counter, and looks out the screen door where a turtle, huge and moss-covered, hunkers out of the slimy ditch to sun itself on a white log. The old man has two teeth and it is difficult to understand him. On the shelves of the little store stand a ring of baloney, a ham, a row of canned goods, two cans of chewing tobacco. That's all. A cooler has twenty cans of soda.

We buy fifteen cans: Barg's Grape and Coke.

While we wait to pay, the old man tells of a black boy who was grabbed by a white mob, tied to a pickup truck, and dragged up and down the street right in front of his store. Finally they tied the bones and raw flesh together in a sack and burned it. "Right by that tree," he says, pointing.

"When was this?" someone asks fearfully.

"Oh, this was just in the late thirties."

Someone breathes a sigh of relief.

For the old man, the others here, it is not only the history that has shaped them; it is the present.

But especially this remains.

Gathered together at Shiloh Missionary Baptist Church on Sunday morning before leaving, twenty tanned faces in a congregation of black. But we belonged. Oh, we belonged there. We were all family now. We knew each other's need and had joined in it. We needed them as much as they needed us.

The choir moved with solemn grace to the tiny choir loft. A large woman in an ocher-colored robe disengaged herself, settled her thick body ponderously at the piano, and let her fingers fly like black jolts of lightning over the keys. We knew the song now, had been singing it all week. We lifted our voices as one with the choir and sang, some of us with tears in our eyes:

> *We are soldiers*
> *in the army,*
> *we have to fight on*
> *even though we cry.*
> *We have to hold up*
> *the bloodstained banner.*
> *We have to hold it up*
> *until we die.*

All the way home the words kept turning in our minds. Over and over someone would begin humming the melody and twenty voices would break out in song. A moment that won't let us go.

So, too, from the start we felt that sense of family at this hospital. We held each other up, and together held up a banner of hope.

Each day at the hospital is carefully scheduled. At first the patient is on a status where he or she must be accompanied by another patient or a nurse to classes and meals. After a few days it became clear that Pat was not suffering from suicidal thoughts; indeed, her longing was to get back to her normal family life. As it became clear that she was fighting hard for this, her therapist permitted her unaccompanied status, allowing her the personal freedom to come and go to classes as she pleased.

At this time her medical team consisted of a staff psychiatrist who headed the team and who was responsible for her medical needs, including prescription of drugs. In addition to the staff nurses, she was assigned to a therapist whom she names as Todd in the journal, and whom she saw on a regular basis, and one nurse called her "special nurse" who was assigned particularly to Pat. Her room, although typically spartan, was a comfortable, large room shared with three other women. It was fronted by large windows overlooking the spacious hospital grounds, and had ample wall space for hanging cards. In time, the walls took on the appearance of a lively wallpaper consisting of cards and pictures. These roommates became very close and dependent upon each other during their short time together.

The normal procedure for a day consisted of a half-hour chapel service in the morning, then a series of classes and activities throughout the day. These varied on a day-to-day basis, but included instructional classes in self-image, assertiveness training, and other practical studies focusing upon the unique individuality of the patient. Secondly, there were classes related to varying forms of therapy, group therapy sessions and psychodrama, for example. In psychodrama, the patients role play their relations with different people in their lives in an effort to understand their own tensions or stresses in relation to these people. This was a very difficult class for Pat to attend. In her situation, she did not have bad or threatening relationships with friends, family, or other relatives, and problems that appeared in the class tended to upset her. Her request for permission not to attend that class was soon reviewed and granted.

In addition, many free-time and group activities were assigned. Craft classes, at levels ranging from making leather moccasins to quite intricate but practical forms of pottery, were always a pleasure. Recognizing the close link between mood and activity, many forms of exercise were also scheduled. This hospital happens to be on spacious grounds that permit a nearly two mile exercise course, but which also includes a gym for competitive sports. Several times a week patients may go out on group activities: a trip to Lake Michigan for swimming, a movie, a shopping trip. Still, all things focus on the illness, and time itself becomes an enemy.

June 27, Thursday. Last night was a frightening night. The overwhelming feeling of depression hit me during the night. I again felt so afraid to take care of Joel, like I would never be able to do that again. I felt nauseated, like my nerves were in knots, and had diarrhea. I lay in bed anyway. At 9:00 A.M. I talked with one of the nurses and I was given some xanax [tranquilizer]. After lying down for an hour and a half I felt some relief. . . . Tears have flowed like rivers today. I feel I've had such a setback. . . . I cry to the Lord and ask for his help and strength. Jean visited at noon. We cried and shared together. She's a special friend. Classes were really hard to get into today. Thankfully they were done by 3:00 P.M. My appetite is poor today. . . . At bedtime I feel a little more relaxed and at peace.

June 29, Saturday. Praise God. I slept well last night and do not feel depressed this morning. Peggy [roommate] and I went down for breakfast together and had a good talk. The ward is real empty. There are only eight women left with about twenty men. During my devotions I copied down some of the precious promises I've clung to these weeks:

1 Peter 5:7, "Cast all your anxieties on Him, for He cares about you."

Isaiah 41:10, "Fear not, for I am with you, be not dismayed, for I am your God. I will strengthen you, I will help you, I will uphold you with my victorious right hand."

Isaiah 26:3, "Thou dost keep him in perfect peace, whose mind is stayed on thee, because he trusts thee."

Philippians 4:6, "Have no anxiety about anything."

Psalm 4:8, "In peace I will both lie down and sleep."

Proverbs 3:5, "Trust in the LORD with all your heart, and do not rely on your own insight."

Philippians 4:19, "And my God will supply every need of yours according to his riches in glory in Christ Jesus."

I called Tim in the morning to make arrangements to go home from 4-7:00 P.M. today. There are very few patients here on the weekend. At 4:00 P.M. Tim came for me. We had grilled hamburgs for supper. They tasted good. Little Joel just sat in his swing. He still is real stuffy from his cold. It seemed wonderful to be home with the children and family. I'm so thankful that the visit went so well. I was able to hold and hug Joel a lot and didn't feel any apprehension or fear as I thought I might. Jeff, Betsy, and Tammy were all so sweet too. I can tell that they've been a big help to Tim. I thank God for this good day and for the care He has given to our family.

Sunday, June 30. I slept soundly with the sleeping pill until 8:00 A.M. After breakfast I realized I was feeling a little down again. . . . I went for a walk alone before lunch. As I sat by the duck pond, I had the feeling that the mother duck could sit on the eggs with no fear or anxiety. So why couldn't I be a mother to Joel without anxiety. . . . I find I cannot think about time because then I become too depressed. I had wanted to meet my wish of being home in two weeks and realize that is unrealistic. My nurse told me the goals I set for myself the past week were too high and that is probably what brought on the depression on Friday.

Monday, July 1. I've been here almost two weeks. . . . Lloyd [a patient] is very upset and depressed today. I will pray for him. As patients we really cry together because we know what the other one feels in the darkness of depression. My blood test from Friday showed my Desipramine level is now at 41 mg/ml in my blood and a therapeutic dose should be 150 mg/ml to 250 mg/ml. It will now be increased to 200 mg in 24 hours instead of 150.

The blood test for the level of antidepressant in the body serves as a clue to Pat's continued up and down state. When prescribing an antidepressant, the physician is guided by several factors including the duration of the depression, its severity, and the contributing factors to the depression. The physician selects from a range of antidepressants that have been demonstrated clinically to be effective for the kind of depression at hand, selecting the one which has the best clinical rate of success. Desipramine, a tricyclic antidepressant, was prescribed for Pat because of its relatively high clinical rate of success for her kind of depression.

Antidepressants are administered in gradual increments to the standard dosage. In this way, the drugs are quite unlike, for example, the familiar penicillin drugs which begin at a standard rate of dosage that is maintained on a regular basis. With antidepressants, the body must adjust to a steadily increasing dosage until the blood tests indicate that the drug has achieved a therapeutic level in the body. The problem here is that each individual has a unique biochemical system. How can we tell whether the drug is in fact working effectively?

The standard maximum dosage for Desipramine is 200 milligrams per twenty-four-hour period. Such a dosage should show a therapeutic presence of the drug in the bloodstream of 150-250 milligrams per milliliter of blood within two to three weeks. When Pat's blood tests showed a level of only 41 milligrams per milliliter of blood, it indicated that she was not responding to the drug nearly as effectively as the doctors wished. Because of the antidepressant she could have "good" days, but they were not consistently good and they could, as the journal entries show, often slip up and down wildly. The drug was failing to stabilize her biochemical system.

Obviously there was a problem here. If the doctors had begun with the drug given the *best* chance of success, a switch to another drug would be to one with a lesser clinical chance of success. Even though it might prove more effective for Pat, the clinical rate of success indicated that it was less likely to do so. This is complicated by the fact that one cannot simply switch an antidepressant overnight. Remember that the dosage is incremental, growing slightly every few days as the body adjusts to it. There are grave medical risks involved in increasing the dosage too quickly. Moreover, in order to switch to another drug, Pat would have to have the dosage of Desipramine gradually *decreased* first. In the same way that one cannot simply take a maximum dosage at once, one also cannot stop taking it at once. The body has to be weaned into and out of the medication.

The situation was further complicated by the fact that Pat had already been hospitalized over two weeks. Clearly her chief longing was to be back at home, united with her loved ones. Just as clearly, her illness was not sufficiently under control to make such a move. No doubt it would work well for a few hours, perhaps even for a day or two. But what would happen if she needed immediate medical attention for an attack of anxiety or depression? If such should happen without proper medical attention, the consequences could be grim indeed.

So it was that some tough decisions had to be made. Steadily, slowly the level of Desipramine would be increased, even if it did not seem to be working as effectively as we hoped. Several weeks later, her dosage was at 400 mg. per day, nearly twice the standard maximum dosage for a person her size and weight. And still the drug had not completely reached a high therapeutic level in the blood counts. Moreover, the higher dosages exacerbated the side effects. For example, Pat, who suffers from allergies, developed severe rashes that would race over her skin, and she would become badly sunburned at the least exposure to the sun. But the physical side effects were manageable. Less easy to handle were the continued ups and downs psychologically. During the good days, Pat was increasingly allowed to spend a few hours out, for a dinner or at home. On the bad days it was impossible.

Wednesday, July 3. *(Joel is 11 weeks today) Our leisure activity was golf, coffee at a restaurant, and going to an antique General Store. I really enjoyed the morning. Today I don't feel depressed at all. I eagerly and confidently look forward to caring for the family again. In creative arts I started working on a ceramic pie dish. I'm sleeping each night without a sleeping pill.*

Friday, July 5. *I awakened feeling well. I met with Todd at 9:30. He spoke with me about thinking about discharge. He wants Tim and me to talk about what my goals will be for the first few days and weeks at home. He said to be very careful to avoid stress and tiredness. He said we must decide together what I will be able to handle each day. My confidence is still low and I feel very dependent upon Tim. . . . This week seemed to pass more quickly than the last one.*

Sunday, July 7. *I didn't have a sleeping pill again at bedtime. I awakened at 5:00 A.M. feeling very depressed— nauseated, diarrhea, tense, and the panicky feeling that I'm not going to get well. And of course the fear that I can't take care of Joel. I called Tim at 9:00 A.M. to tell him I can't come home because of the way I feel. I can't stop crying. At 9:15 the nurse gave me a xanax. For a half hour I still feel sad and hopeless, then gradually I'm able to relax and fall asleep for an hour. I feel so guilty that I can't seem to get well. I feel like a stranger to myself when I feel this way. I can't read my Bible or pray—I know God knows my needs and the needs of my family and I trust He will take care of us all. I've reread my favorite Bible promises. But I can't feel them right now. . . . I feel so lonely, so fearful, and like such a failure. It's like depression is a monster which comes out of nowhere and attacks. I feel like a child again, so dependent upon everyone. . . .*

Monday, July 8. *I awaken feeling less depressed, but that depression leaves me feeling so afraid. It's like I'm afraid it will pop out again, and I wonder if my confidence will ever return. The doctor saw me and said he was going to increase my*

*Desipramine to 300 mg. per day. If the rash gets worse, I'll
have to change to something else.*

It was a good thing we didn't know this: the situation
was to get worse before it would get better.

We don't understand these things. We are, as David
said, "fearfully and wonderfully made." Wonderful, yes.
We are made unique: God has a plan for each one of us
whom he has made. But also fearfully: we don't always
understand the persons we are. Sometimes the dark
imperfection blinds us to the light of wonder.

6 Grasping a Lifeline: Nurturing the Troubled Family

F or several years a handbell choir called The Joyful Noise had practiced every week. It isn't a large group, maybe twenty members. Surprisingly, for a group which isn't very large, they have a director and five assistants. Perhaps they practiced so hard and long because they wanted to be thoroughly professional. They wanted to meet their own hard and high standards of perfection before their first public concert.

Our church had the good blessing to be selected for the first public performance of The Joyful Noise. They would provide a half hour concert during the regular evening worship service.

I imagine it was a bit intimidating to the choir members. Our church is packed wall to wall, including folding chairs set up in aisles, for its evening worship services. But they had practiced long and they certainly appeared confident. Nonetheless, from where I sat just three rows from the front, I detected a kind of nervous tension in the air. First performances, after all, don't occur every day. The choir members filed in, smiling happily at the full church. Four or five of them jostled for space in their wheelchairs. Oh yes, in addition to their hard practices and their demanding standards, The Joyful Noise Handbell Choir members have one other thing in common. They are all handicapped.

I spotted him right off. There's one in every crowd—a cut-up. He jostled his neighbors, turned around and beamed at the congregation, shuffled restlessly in the pew. And why shouldn't he be proud? This was the first public performance.

The time came. The choir arranged itself across the front of the sanctuary. Wheelchairs were moved into positions in the front. The director introduced them after having positioned her five assistants among them. She asked the congregation for patience if they hit wrong notes. She didn't have to ask. The first number went smoothly. A boy with cerebral palsy in one of the wheelchairs loudly clanged, with help from one of the assistants, an "Amen" with the big bell. The congregation applauded resoundingly.

Still there was some of that nervous tension. You could feel it in the congregation. Things had gone well indeed on the first number. Not that we're a highbrow congregation, expecting perfection on every note. Far from it. But you could sense the congregation feeling for the performers. It had gone well. But how long . . . ?

That applause was all he needed, this cut-up. Garbed in his red choir gown, he began flashing his white-gloved hands to his ears, flapping them happily. Yes, the nervousness I detected rose appreciably. When his turn came to ring the big bell, he warmed up by winding his arm like Dwight Gooden preparing his fast ball. People in the front row were prepared to duck. But he held on. He clanged that large bell gloriously, providing an ear-shattering note that shivered the rafters. Before the note could die out, this cut-up clapped the huge bell to his neighbor's ear. The man next to him, whose ear had suffered the indignity, rolled his eyes awesomely and threatened to pass out, but he managed to come back with his own note, slightly late.

At the end of the number the cut-up broke into an enormous grin, dancing happily, if precariously, on the chancel steps.

The nervousness broke like a dam under a floodtide of joy. People laughed and clapped. Something happened: We joined the Joyful Noise in rejoicing. We were one. We were David dancing before the Lord with all his might; Michal had disappeared. I have seldom spent a happier hour in a church than that night.

It is harder to enter into a person's sorrow. But no less important. The Joyful Noise needed to perform *before* someone, and we needed to rejoice *with* them. So too, the family in need needs others to enter into their need with them. When the music is all broken, the harmonies distorted and the tune lost, we need others to enter in to show the way back to rejoicing.

In passages from Pat's journal, one sees over and over that she expresses her greatest fear for her family. Indeed, it was a legitimate fear that surfaced in several ways. Since Pat, as primary nurturer in the structure of our family, was apart from the family, all those traditional areas of mothering seemed in jeopardy. The familiar routines of washing clothes, preparing meals, keeping schedules, providing close physical contact, and directing activities were now askew. Moreover, her greatest fear, perhaps, lay simply in this: What if someone needs that special mother's touch—the hurt to be soothed, the word of encouragement? A family moves to a finely tuned, if highly flexible, harmony. Now the lead director was absent.

The feeling intensified as the weeks progressed by the brief visits we had together as a family. Even as we met, this thought was in our minds: In so many minutes or hours we will have to part again. Uncertainty and impermanence seemed to be the fundamental conditions of our family. Order, then, was the compelling need.

Over and over others asked us, "What can I do to help?" From our experience, six primary areas emerge that warrant the attention of the Christian community seeking to help the family in need.

1. *Prayer Support*

At one time or another, we all experience those points in life where events are so hectic or so unsettling that we seem too busy to pray. Or we reach those points in our lives where living itself seems a kind of prayer, when we almost constantly throw our prayers before God's grace, when we say: God knows and understands. So let it be. Twice before in my life I had reached such points, and they helped me understand my attitude toward and belief in prayer during this time.

The first time was when I was drafted out of graduate school into the army. I wanted to be a teacher. Now suddenly a hole was carved in my plans and I was overwhelmed by events so baffling to me, so utterly beyond my experience or comprehension that I didn't know how to pray about them. Yes, I prayed. But the prayers were urgent appeals as my life changed in a whirlpool of events. It seemed to me that my prayers were pleas wrenched from a confused mind. My solace at the time was the fact that others were praying for me, interceding on my behalf. But how I longed to still the engine of my life, to meditate apart from the noise and hurry of events, to be still and know that He is God.

The second event arose a few years ago. Our youngest daughter, Tammy, then four years of age, was to have extensive thoracic surgery to reconstruct her chest cavity. The fears were so numbing that I found it difficult to pray, to coherently articulate my fears into prayer. Then, too, I clung to the verses from Philippians 4:6-7: "Have no anxiety about anything, but in everything by prayer and supplication with thanksgiving let your requests be made known to God. And the peace of God, which passes all understanding, will keep your hearts and your minds in Christ Jesus."

We were in the surgical waiting room of a large metropolitan hospital. The surgery was delayed several times, and finally began in the early afternoon. The procedure was to take several hours. Slowly the clock ticked the minutes off. The waiting room emptied as other surgeries finished. Midway through the afternoon, our pastor arrived. We talked quietly in a corner of the room.

Suddenly, a dozen supercharged, nearly hysterical people milled into the room. Moans mingled with piercing cries of anguish. The phone was in hot use. Through the steady weeping of some older women in the group, urgent cries from the person monitoring the phone shot out through the room.

"June Ann! You got any more quarters?"

"Anyone got quarters? Got to phone Abner!"

Someone found quarters.

"Abner got to be here. Phone Abner."

"That's right. Call Lucille. Lucille got to know." And as the phone blistered under the summonses, more people milled into the room.

Their daughter, niece, sister—a police officer—had been shot in a courtroom by a prisoner who had somehow seized a guard's weapon. The noise became deafening. A reporter rushed into the room asking questions

of anyone he could corner. The weeping rose to a cre-
scendo.

We were a lonely party there, enduring the long probing of our daughter's thoracic cavity under the surgeon's
knife, now entering the fourth hour. Quietly we bowed
our heads. Our pastor began to pray with us.

Silence fell suddenly on that room like an eerie blan-
ket. As our pastor's voice rose in prayer, it rose to include
the need of all those others in the room also. At the end
of the prayer there was not a dry eye in that room. Hearts
had been knit together in our common need laid before
the throne of God. We were one people; one in our need
for God.

Other such times have arisen in my life, times when
prayers turn to pleas, when fears throttle the conscious
praying mind so that only a groan of longing slips
through. Such a time struck again during Pat's illness,
in a way I had never experienced before.

I was mindful of it the first night our pastor stopped
by our house, just after Pat had been admitted. He asked,
"Would you like me to announce this to the congregation, to ask them to pray for you and Pat?"

"Of course," I said. "Please do."

The fact that he raised it as a question, however, was
puzzling. I understand it now. For many years depression has been the secret illness, something one was
deeply ashamed of. It was seen as a weakness rather
than an illness. People talked about depression with
bowed heads and averted faces. Maybe one or two close
friends were asked to pray; for the others there was a
deep silence. So and so has some "problem."

If nothing else, this book intends to lay that belief to
rest. We must be honest about this illness.

Prayers for Pat and for our family became regular parts
of the congregational prayer. (Our church regularly includes personal needs of its members in congregational

prayer. Moreover, our congregation has a prayer-chain in which needs are telephoned to those committed to regular intercessory prayer.) At a time when one finds it difficult to pray, because of anxieties, pressures, or uncertainties, that person needs a body of committed believers lifting up those anxieties, pressures, and uncertainties to the Lord.

2. *Maintain Routines*

The family in need also has practical needs. My own primary concern was for care of our baby and children. Friends of the older children jumped in immediately to help them. Someone would take them swimming for a day. Another would invite them to a cottage for a day. This was important. As much as I and the children needed to stay together as a family unit—and we did become tremendously dependent upon each other—the children still needed activities of their own.

My greatest need as a father and fumbling, role-playing mother, however, was with baby Joel. I was caught in a half dozen different directions, and I also needed some time to myself. The first intervention came the day I had my regular softball game. Can one appreciate the significance of that simple item? One has to understand that I'd rather play softball than eat. I love softball. I grew up playing softball for hours each day during summers. I can't remember ever having held something in my hand without wanting to throw it. This is more than a sport to me; it's a passion.

I haven't made this love very secret. I talk softball or baseball with anyone I can find willing to listen. Before he died, my eighty-year-old neighbor and I saw each other every morning to run through the last night's Tigers game. While we talked, I would pitch stones at the oak trees in the back yard to make a point. If someone walked into our house they would have to find their way through a litter of balls. Softballs, baseballs, tennis balls, racquetballs—they're always in use and seldom neatly on shelves. Nearly any evening in the summer the kids and I are at the park across the street working up a game, one that can include the youngest child and anyone else who wanders by.

I feel right at home, then, on my church softball team whose members share my passion. Indeed, we keep it in perspective. But how good it is to start that first practice in early April, when in Michigan the snow has hardly cleared from the ground. The sweet smack of the bat on cowhide calls in Spring. And even though we joke about being the "over the hill gang," we have won league championships in two of the last three years. My teammates are no different than I. We schedule vacations around softball games.

So it was that when Thursday of Pat's first week of hospitalization rolled around, I awakened with the sinking knowledge that I would miss the game . . . and how many after that? What strange creatures we humans are. My wife was in the hospital. Exams lay on the desk to be graded. The baby was insisting upon his bottle in no uncertain terms. And I staggered out of bed upset because I would miss a ball game? Strange but true. How sweet it was, then, when our friend, Nancy, called about the time I got the bottle plugged in.

"You have a ball game tonight, don't you? What time is it?"

"Yeah, I guess so. Ball game's at seven."

"Well, I'll be over at six to watch Joel. You need to go to your game."

I did little dance steps all over the kitchen—among the unpicked-up toys, a few dirty clothes, and of course, a few loose balls.

Here is the second important area of need. When a family's routine is wrenched awry, it is necessary to help restore order by providing time for those routines. It may be a small matter like making sure someone gets to a ball game, or a Bible study, or to church services. But these are necessary. They remind us of who we are, of a certain order that invests our lives with peace. I didn't miss a ball game during that whole summer. Our friends knew it was important that I didn't. Important for whom? The world wouldn't end if I didn't play ball. We all knew that. But it was important for my well-being. I thank God for friends who remembered that.

Routines that mark the commonplace, the normal motions of our lives, must be guarded, not to deny the reality of the illness but to affirm the reality of lovingkindness. It might be as simple as taking the children of the family on a shopping trip, or to a lake or recreation area. It might mean asking the spouse if there is some special activity that person wants to be free to do. These are small items, but they signal a bond of communal caring.

3. *Providing Child Care*

The third area represented my greatest personal need, but also a crisis of sorts for me. Thrust suddenly into the role of primary nurturer for an infant, I was amazed at several things. First of all, I really, truly loved caring for the baby. I have never been one of those males squeamish of diapers, leaping out of the house when the baby decides to spit up, leery of runny noses. I don't know how to explain this, but I have always enjoyed participating in the care of each of our children. And I'm grateful for that. It has had its good results.

I have noticed, now that I have two of them and one standing eagerly on the threshold, that teenagers are unusual creatures, kind of an alien race unwillingly visiting the planet for about half a dozen years before the real person inhabits that changing body again. Teenagers are human, of course; we just haven't figured out how they fit into the human race. Now, one trait of this syndrome that I have noticed is that overnight—it happens the night before the thirteenth birthday—these people change from uninhibited, even exhibitionist persons to the most private creatures on the face of the earth. In our home it was signaled by signs first of all. They hang on a bedroom door: PLEASE KNOCK. PRIVATE. And suddenly they want diaries (with a lock, please!) for birthday presents, and they hide their yearbooks in some secret place, usually under the pile of unwashed clothes in the corner of their closets. There are other signs. For example, they come home from school and rampage through the cupboards eating everything in sight like a plague of locusts. But when you open their knapsacks, the school lunch isn't eaten. Why do they get hungry at 3:30 P.M., and not before? And they discover a strange language, incomprehensible to adults. A certain teacher is a "diz." A certain boy may be a "quaz" or "coooool." These are minor signs, however. The primary one is privacy.

Suddenly these bodies that used to walk around the house in any stage of undress are locked into steamy bathrooms for primping and secret rituals of beautifying. Strange ointments purchased with allowances suddenly appear. The closed door becomes the greatest prize. When I once walked into the bathroom by mistake upon one of my partially-clad teenagers, I was met with a heated barrage: "Can't I have privacy, Dad? Let me get dressed in peace!" Yes, except that it takes half the morning when I have to shave—and the hot water is long gone. I reminded my indignant teenager, "Listen, I changed your dirty diapers when you were a baby! Think about that."

I did shut the door. But I felt I had the upper hand.

There is a huge difference, however, between participating in childcare and being the primary nurturer. And I now knew that difference well . . . and its demands. The problem was that there were so many other demands. Some were obvious, such as the needs of the other children. It would be easy to ignore those needs. They were old enough to fend for themselves if they had to. But they shouldn't have to. However, they were less dependent upon me, and I could meet their needs largely by providing some semblance of order and routine in the house and by encouraging them to live as normally as possible; that is, to keep dates for special activities, visiting friends, and so forth.

A second obvious need was for me to maintain regular visits with Pat, and to make sure the children had the opportunity to visit. From the first day I determined that I would see Pat, however briefly, every day. It was fully as important to me as to her. During the week I would often try to take one or two of the children along, and at least once a week I tried to take all the children along to visit or eat a meal at the hospital with her.

The greatest focus of immediate need, however, was the baby, who was now totally dependent upon my care. The crisis arose from this fact: The primary nurturer in the home also has needs. Fortunately, others recognized this fact—but in such a way that a crisis arose in me.

It began subtly. Both of our parents live within an easy drive of our home, and both helped willingly. For example, one morning a week, I gave over the household care to one of our mothers. The first thing I would do, very early, would be to go out for a good breakfast at a restaurant, leisurely enjoying the meal while reading a newspaper. Then up to my office, that place where I had spent so many hours and where I now seemed virtually a stranger. How good it was to have a cup of coffee with colleagues, to catch up on correspondence, to take care of accumulated details. This made me mindful of how absolutely essential for the primary nurturer to have such free time—to do nothing, or what he or she pleases. In fact, I am convinced that the most important thing a husband can do for a new mother is to insure that she gets out one or two mornings a week to do just that—whatever she wants.

As welcome as this help was, as the days stretched into weeks it was insufficient. Joel still hadn't slept a night through. The daily demands and needs escalated. Here's where the crisis came. And it came in a most generous offer. My sister-in-law called and simply told me that she was taking Joel for the weekend. No, not for a morning. For a weekend. And that was a crisis. I knew I should—that I had to—do it. I had to meet those other needs, including my own which at this point consisted mainly of a good night's sleep. But here was this baby who, I believed, was totally, absolutely dependent upon me.

For the first time I fully understood Pat's feelings. For the first time *I entered into them*. They became mine. Was I letting my baby down? Had I failed?

Nonetheless, my sister-in-law insisted. Not only did it work marvelously for everyone involved—in fact, for the first time Joel slept through the night and would every night thereafter—I discovered that the world would go along just fine if I relaxed. Oh, but I had to fight the feelings of failure. I could not, and would not, have done it without that insistence. Thereafter, every week my sister or sister-in-law shared turns taking the baby for a night or two. It was important, I believe, that it wasn't all the time. I still needed to feel in control. But I also had to relinquish some responsibility.

As I began to realize this, I also began to realize that I had been receiving dozens of phone calls from church members and friends offering to take care of the baby or the other children. They made sure that I had free time each evening to visit Pat, and that I had blocks of time to be free myself, to rest, to run errands, to go to my office.

In fact, I found that I had to develop a balance of gratitude and frankness in dealing with this. I kept a weekly calendar and carefully scheduled the childcare. It would be easy to schedule myself out of the picture. It was necessary that I didn't—that no family in need does so. The children still needed me as primary nurturer and the bearer of authority and responsibility. When the blocks of time that I had scheduled were filled, I felt perfectly free to ask those who offered if I could schedule them as back-up help in case of an emergency. Furthermore, I tried to schedule one person at regular times, so that the baby and the children had established routines instead of simply being "dumped" here or there.

One of the good effects of this experience is that Joel developed a rare willingness to go anywhere and to be with anyone. One of my fondest recollections from a not very fond time is this. Certain friends of ours have a spacious backyard with a large pool. Several times during the summer we get together there with friends for a cook-out and swimming party. We had had one such evening scheduled before Pat was hospitalized. Even though I was going to visit her on that evening, our friends insisted that the children, including Joel, come to the party. I dropped them all off and Pat and I enjoyed a wonderful evening at a restaurant together. When I arrived after dark to pick up the children, I noticed that a rocking chair had been brought out to the pool deck. There, one of our friends was cuddling Joel, softly singing "Jesus Loves Me" to him as he nodded on her shoulder and while others splashed noisily in the pool. When it was time to leave, one of the mothers protested, "I haven't had my turn yet!" Each of them had taken a long turn at rocking and singing to him. Seldom has a baby had such care.

And it was necessary care—for the baby as well as for

me and the other children. The third area of need we observe, then, is the need for child care to free the spouse to meet other needs or simply to enjoy some free time. I don't know how we could have survived as a family without it.

4. *Mom's Home Cooking*

As a college teacher, I enjoy the anticipation in my students as Thanksgiving vacation approaches. A tremendous jumble of emotions runs through their minds, but somehow it all centers on mom's home cooking. They have had it with cafeteria meals. Their mouths are watering for their dream meals of home.

I sometimes thought that our meals during this period were very much like a cafeteria. Each one of us had his or her own wishes, and we concocted some of the wildest meals imaginable. Our blessing lay in the fact that there is a home delivery pizza house just two blocks away. Night after night, it seemed, six o'clock would roll around and I would discover that I didn't have anything for dinner. Chalk up another one for the pizza house.

Enter a group of people from the church who had established a congregation-wide network to provide for just such needs. One person coordinated a schedule. Therefore, if anyone who was not a member of our church called me to offer a meal, I could steer that person to the coordinator for scheduling. This is important, for the meals brought to a family in need can range from an overabundance for a few days to none at all for a few days. It is, quite simply, poor Christian stewardship—of goods and time—to work without a schedule. I have seen the regrettable circumstance where families were inundated with so much food that they had to throw some out. Also, a coordinator can tailor a menu to family tastes. Each family has favorites—or the opposite. But even a favorite can fail if it appears four nights in a row.

The first step in this process began when the coordinator met with me. Briefly we discussed scheduling and we decided that meals should be brought in three evenings a week—Monday, Wednesday, and Friday. That was realistic for me. I didn't want meals every night. If there were leftovers, I could freeze them and have them another night. Also I knew that some people would simply drop something off on the spur of the moment, and I wanted to respect that principle of stewardship. I can't stand to throw out food, and I knew by now how much work was involved to prepare it. We also talked a bit about our favorite foods in case people inquired about that, and the best time for delivery. Finally, and perhaps most importantly, the coordinator told me when the dishes would be picked up and returned so that I wouldn't have to worry about that time-consuming task.

Having established these fundamental "ground rules" with the coordinator, the system worked marvelously. Many people still dropped off snacks on their own initiative, and they were much appreciated. Cookies and such are easily frozen for later use, but they also have a way of disappearing in a hurry. The important thing here was that we had a regular schedule imposed upon us. Things were not left to chance.

I began to look forward to those deliveries for another reason. Few other events were as quietly meaningful for me. With the hectic demands of playing house-father, it was a wonderful relief simply to chat with other adults for a few minutes, to hear their simple words of reassurance and concern, to know that we had a wide support network. That contact meant wholly as much to me as the meals themselves.

5. *Financial Need*

Here is a hard thing to talk about, but we cannot afford to be anything less than honest and realistic here. Since that is the case, let me be frank. Even brief medical illnesses can be expensive. Prolonged ones can be devastating. Ones for psychiatric illnesses overwhelming.

The hospital costs in themselves are simply so astonishing that the family living on a budget is inclined to simply let them wash over as an unreality. These figures can't be right. Two hundred and some dollars for each day of hospitalization? Two to three hundred dollars a week for medication and tests? Haven't they heard of generic drugs? Hundreds of dollars for therapy and classes. Don't they have any two-for-the-price-of-one plan, or a "Tuesday Special"? The sums are staggering. But they are made even more so by the fact that most health insurance policies provide woefully inadequate coverage for psychiatric illnesses.

We were fortunate in our situation that Pat's hospitalization fell under the major medical rider to our policy. As such, nearly all of the costs of the hospitalization were paid in full by the policy. Our alternative would have been to take out a long-term loan nearly equivalent to our mortgage. Even so, there were dozens of hidden costs beyond the amount we did have to pay for the hospitalization and drugs. What are these?

For one thing, there was a tremendous amount of travel between the hospital and home. I was filling up the gas tank more than once a week. There were the follow-up costs for outpatient therapy and medicines. Maybe I should add all those pizzas. These made a small dent in the budget. Nonetheless, I was astonished to find, when I did my year-end taxes for that year, that medical costs totaled nearly 20 percent of my total income. However, when the deacons from our church stopped by to inquire about our financial need, which they did several times, I was honestly and thankfully able to tell them that God was meeting our need.

This is not always the case. Medical costs are frightfully high and the need for financial support is urgent in many families. This support may be offered in several ways. If the church is to assist financially, I believe it is usually best to do so by paying specific bills, be they medical, food, utility payments, or other such specific needs. The church should maintain some degree of specific accountability for good stewardship. This is not to say that the church might not ever give a cash gift to a family in need, but it is a wiser and more responsible course of action to pay specific bills that the family cannot handle.

The situation may differ with financial gifts from individuals within the church community. In our church family, for example, we have had periods where heads of families have lost employment. Several times this has happened to close friends of ours. We see it as a gesture of our Christian friendship to personally give them, or mail to them in a note, a check to help with general expenses. It may simply be a case of giving the parents enough money to go out for dinner. In such cases, we don't ask first if the family needs the money. We simply give it and insist they receive it as a token of our love for them.

We find an analogy here with another event: friends mourning the death of a loved one. More than once, Pat and I have wondered, as we have gone to the funeral home to console the bereaved, whether such a visit is really necessary or appreciated. Sometimes these visits are to people whom we really don't know very well. But never once have we left the funeral home when we didn't feel that our visit was important. Never once. The same kind of pattern can hold in benevolence. It is better to make the offer than to wonder if it is really needed.

6. *Visiting the Ill Person*

I have saved the most difficult help for the family in need for last. It is a sensitive discussion. People have hard questions in their minds. "Am I able to visit a mental hospital? Will he or she really want to see me? I don't know what to say. Will it make me depressed?"

The quick answers are these. You *can* visit the mental hospital. You simply get in your car and go. Yes, the patient very much wants to see you, even if he or she acts otherwise. In fact, that person might ask you to leave after a few minutes, but that has nothing to do with you and doesn't mean that your visit is unappreciated. Yes, it is hard to know what to say. But how do we talk with anyone? A depressed person doesn't stop being human. No, you won't catch depression. It is an illness, not a communicable disease. But remember, even if the visit has made you feel sad, confused, or angry, it has been important to the patient.

Those are the quick answers to the hard questions. They are insufficient, as so many of our attitudes about depression are. Visits with the patient, both in the hospital and later in the home, are so important that we want to consider them more carefully. Remember that the depressed person feels of little worth and also very alone. It is the nature of the illness. A visit can knock a little light of the reality of love into that dark feeling. Since people commonly have some fears about such visits, we have a few practical suggestions and cautions to guide them.

The first caution has to be stated negatively: *Don't Play Psychiatrist.* The purpose of your visit is not to solve the patient's problems. You can't do that, and trying to do so will only confuse the patient. The world of psychiatric illnesses is clouded with popular and religious misunderstanding. For example, some people insist on seeing depression as the result of a sin (cause). If the sin can be named and exorcised, the patient will get well. I believe *that* attitude is a sin. It is judgmental and wrong.

Or, we may bring quick remedies that help us over the "blues." When the clinically depressed person tries them, they don't work. The failure will only heighten the sense of depression.

Similar to this error of bringing quick cures is the effort to share problems to create a sense of common identity or intimacy with the patient. The exception to this, as I will point out later, is people who have experienced depression themselves, who know the blackness of the sea, and who can share the promise of recovery. In this case the patient is also provided with a goal and a hope. As a general guide the depressed person desperately needs encouragement. He or she needs to be told, over and over again, *you will get well*.

The positive counterpart of this lesson is to encourage the depressed person. She really believes she will never get well, and she needs the emphatic encouragement of others that indeed she will. Such encouragement should be offered simply and sincerely, not as a cheerleader directing emotions, but as a loving, supportive friend who believes the encouragement.

This negative caution and positive direction has been ably stated by Ray Grissen in an article titled "Coping with Depression." Here Grissen comments on visits made during his wife's hospitalization, and while he applies it specifically to ministerial visits the point applies generally:

> Many ministers must learn—as I learned—
> that depression is sickness. My wife shared a
> room with another patient who also had tum-
> bled into the black pit of despair. Intending
> to cheer her, her minister said, "No one has
> ever died from this." She replied bitterly, "I
> know. I wish I could." Equally disastrous is
> the well-meant advice to a patient to lay her
> burdens before the Lord to find peace for her
> soul. Preaching at a depressed person is not
> a prescription that profits. Does a minister
> comfort with a lecture a person suffering from

cancer or diabetes? Hardly. Admonition, sincere though it may be, essentially denies that depression is illness. Ministers help best when they allow the person to be ill and not merely out of tune with the Lord.

The quiet, steady, non-condemning presence of the minister also provides a comfort that cannot be voiced. I recall our minister's response when my wife hesitantly admitted that she had quit praying because God didn't listen to her anyway. "That's all right," comforted Rev. Henry De Mott, "because we are all praying for you. That's what fellow believers are for." When an agonizing question pops up, a minister's solid insight is like a rope flung to a drowning swimmer. He can bless the sick person with a tug of strength as she flounders in the murky waters of self-accusation, guilt, and hopelessness.[29]

A second caution warns the visitor against making comparative statements, those offhand remarks that reveal to the patient the gulf between his or her present state and the normal world, or that enforce the patient's concept of unworthiness in comparison to the lives of others. A rather extreme example of this came to my attention recently. A neighbor has suffered from multiple sclerosis for some years, an illness now so severe that he has been committed to the care of a nursing home. His wife was with him one day when a visitor, in an effort to be jovial, no doubt, blurted out: "Boy! You have the life just relaxing in that wheelchair all day." That comment, which we would regard as a matter of incredibly poor taste, cut to the heart of this man who would do anything to walk again. Another time, this same man received a visitor who gave a long, detailed accounting of a Florida vacation. The patient had to be content seeing the winter snows through his window. How he would have loved to build a snowman with his children once again.

A rule of common sense operates here. A visitor doesn't have to be wise or witty, nor entertain with personal adventures. This doesn't mean, of course, that the visitor never laughs or never speaks of personal experiences. Indeed, one of Pat's most prized visitors was a colleague of mine whose unstoppable laughter is so infectious that people begin to smile when he walks in the room. The visitor does have some obligation, however, to place himself in the patient's shoes for a short time, and to be sympathetic to the need at hand.

Having observed the negative caution not to play psychiatrist, we want to stress, secondly, the positive value of visiting the depressed person. That person does need visits. Understand that she may not feel like talking. She may even have to ask you to leave if she's not feeling well. Don't let that discourage you. Even in such a situation the depressed person is very mindful of the fact that someone cared enough to come out to see her. The action itself is important and meaningful. It is helpful to call before a visit to make sure that the person is available or that the patient is able to visit. At certain points Pat simply didn't feel up to a visit, in much the same way that a person who is physically ill might not.

Visits should continue after the hospitalized patient returns home. As we shall see in another chapter, the initial return to home is a very vulnerable and fragile time for the depressed person. An invitation to go out for coffee or lunch, or even a quick visit at home, is very important.

If you simply can't arrange a visit, however, you can send a card. The highlight of Pat's day, and for every patient on her ward, was mail time. A simple card with a short, penned note can be very meaningful. All the patients on Pat's ward hung their cards on the walls around their beds. The rooms had the liveliest wallpaper around. Some people would send cards every few days to remind Pat that they were thinking of and praying for her.

Assuming, then, that you do arrange a visit with a depressed person, what do you talk about? Remember that your presence itself is important. You might sit quietly for a few minutes, or go for a walk. Don't be afraid of silences. Remember above all that however depressed, the patient is still a person. That person has all the hopes, fears, dreams, expectations that you do. If the patient has classes—a normal hospital routine— inquire about them. If he or she is working on a craft, ask to see it. You might have questions of your own about medications and their effects. Feel free to ask. Ask about chapel services, if such are held. These are things at the center of the patient's life, and it is good to inquire about them. If the patient volunteers to talk about how she is feeling, let her. Generally, I would not encourage questions about the state of feeling, unless you have known the patient well and have seen her often enough to understand the fluctuations of her psychological condition. Surely we do not mean by this that the condition is to be ignored or denied, but that it is frequently best not to let it become a matter of prolonged discussion. In depression, the patient often cannot see beyond feelings, and it is helpful to direct attention along different avenues.

I should add that I always asked Pat about her feelings, as the first item during our visits. It was absolutely necessary that she be able to confide in me and know that I was concerned about her. Very quickly, however, we would be chatting about other things. Generally, I would suggest to visitors that if the patient wants to talk about his or her feelings, you listen sympathetically and respond by holding those feelings up to God in a brief prayer.

And, yes, do feel free to pray with the patient, and to read a *brief* passage of Scripture. The patient needs this connecting, supportive link with God affirmed by others. Pray directly in intercession for the patient, mentioning specific needs or concerns that have come up in your discussion.

Don't become upset when the patient cries with you. That's when they need you most. He or she might want to be held, or to hold your hand. But let the patient cry. You can excuse yourself when the patient begins to collect herself, but don't dart out the moment she starts crying. Such an action will be construed as rejection. Understand that the patient cannot fully control crying spells while depressed, and that it is a health-bringing emotional release for her.

In relation to that, you should recognize that just as depression is unique to the person's individual experience of it, so too the depressed person may fluctuate in mood. On one visit the patient may talk freely; on the next, she may maintain a glassy silence. On one visit the patient may want you to pray with him; on the next, he may prefer a quiet walk. Hence the importance of merely making yourself available. Scripted performances don't work very well. Feel free to let the spirit of the relationship and the Holy Spirit guide you.

Perhaps some of the most helpful visits for Pat were those paid by people who had formerly been ill with depression. Three women in particular, each of whom had been hospitalized with depression in the past, made regular visits with Pat. They could identify with her moods (the visits must have been difficult for them), and they could also provide her a model of recovery, the assurance that she would get well and function normally again.

Lastly, encourage, encourage, encourage. Tell the

patient over and over that she will get well and that she is making progress. Promise that you will keep praying for her because you know God will make her well again. The depressed person is something like a dry well: the self-image and self-respect have simply run dry. Now there is only this husk through which tears and fears wander. We can begin to fill that well by pouring encouragement by the bucketful into it, by nurturing the springs of living water with prayer, by striving to make the hope flow again.

7 Steps toward the Shore: The Way Home

Walk past the magazine counter of any store, and you will see slick periodicals heralding the latest beauty breakthroughs. The human face is the prominent cover photo. Magazines for teenagers through the elderly tout make-up secrets that will rivet attention on the eyes, skin, lips, or teeth. To be common is a crime; to be less than perfect a woeful shortcoming. We have to dazzle, make people turn and stare. And most of the attention in the billion-dollar industry of cosmetics focuses upon facial features. Beauty editors debate which feature attracts the most attention in order to inform their audiences how to seduce the stares and attraction of lesser mortals.

In this world of dazzle I remain a kind of oddity. When I meet someone, my attention doesn't linger first of all upon a glittering smile, although I like happy people and appreciate a warm smile. It doesn't rest first of all upon eyes, unless they possess a particularly unusual paint job, the artistry of which I want to study for a moment. But I do like people who look me in the eye. My attention often comes to rest, oddly enough, upon a person's hands. I don't mean just the handshake, although I also confess that I like a firm grip from women or men. The focus rests upon the hands themselves.

In the person's hands you can count the tracery of a life. They are indicators of a person's soul, a map of events, a record of beauty that comes not from cosmetics but from the way a person has worked and endured and rejoiced. I find these things in a person's hands.

One can read this testament first of all in the way people use their hands in relation to the rest of their body. Hands thrust deeply into pockets or clenched to a chest tell me something about the way a person lives a life. Hands raised in praise during a worship service tell something about a person's spirit. In our church we often conclude services with a praise offering in song to the Lord. Many members raise their hands with their voices as they glorify Jesus.

For the past six months, at the time of this writing, we have been taking three formerly unchurched children, in addition to our own four, to our Sunday school and worship services. It started as a way to help the parents who had given birth to a severely handicapped infant and who needed some time to themselves. It was easy enough for us to take the three older children on Sundays, to pick them up in the morning and keep them with us for the day.

The children, especially the youngest—six-year-old Sara—had dozens of questions that they would raise over dinner following the service. But we could tell that they were puzzled by this matter of lifting hands. The only experience they had with it had been in school, where they raised a hand in response to a teacher's question. But where was the question here? Finally, upon leaving a worship service one morning, Sara tugged on

Pat's arm.

"Pat," she asked, "how come everyone here knows the answer and I don't?" *There's* a rich analogy.

But this attention I have to hands is more than simply how people use them. It is a fascination with the hands themselves. They are the hardest working members of our body, a miracle of nerves and muscles and tendons, and yet we pay them scant attention. While a few people carefully tend inch-long talons, a kind of horticulture of the nail, most of us are content to clip the nails every other week or so.

In the rough ridges of tendons and veins lies a map of a person's years. In the muscled wrists lies a testimony to labor given. In the cracked calluses lies a revelation of those things a person has striven with and against. Since I have written the first drafts of all of my manuscripts in longhand, the middle fingers of my right hand are permanently bent and ridged to the grip of a pen. In the hand you can find the stresses and strains of a life, the broken and bent fingers, the satiny smooth or roughly spotted skin.

When I think of such hands, a picture returns again and again to my mind—the hands of my father at the keyboard of the piano. He was a gifted baseball player in his youth; he pitched for many years until he threw out his arm and had to shift to shortstop. I can see those years in his hands; the fingers bend and curl to the shape of cowhide. One finger is broken and crooks inward from where a hard liner smashed into it. It seems odd to find *those* hands at the keyboard, stroking melodies from the piano. But that is how I remember them in this picture from my mind.

I guess he took lessons somewhere in his youth, but mostly he played by ear—songs that live in the heart instead of the head—melodies that flow along the blood's pulsing and emerge through the crooked fingertips. And this song, above all others, I remember him playing. I hear it now as if he were seated there once again. And I remember the words of that old song, for often I would voice them from another room while he played:

> *In shady green pastures, so rich and so sweet,*
> *God leads his dear children along;*
> *Where the water's cool flow bathes the*
>   *weary one's feet,*
> *God leads his dear children along.*
> *Some through the waters, some through the flood,*
> *Some through the fire, but all through the blood;*
> *Some through great sorrow, but God gives a song,*
> *In the night season and all the day long.*[30]

These are the words of God's promise in Isaiah 43—the words that kept working through my mind during this time we walked through the waters and the flood. And they came also with the image of Pat's hands, her calm, ministering hands, often wrung now in the cold anxiety of her illness.

We were in the flood during these weeks, and the tide seemed to boil harder rather than recede. Pat had now passed over the original projection of a three-week hospitalization and yet we found no steady improvement in her condition. Former roommates were discharged; new ones came. With each day the homesickness and loneliness grew. Thus the tension between the lack of improvement and longing to be home increased. Now on open leave status, Pat could spend a day or two at home on the weekends, but each time she had to return. At three weeks we begin to notice this pronounced tension in her journal entries.

July 9 (three weeks). This morning I awakened feeling very homesick and also very lonely for the children and Tim. I prayed for each of them individually and had many tears of loneliness.

I ate fair at breakfast and poorly at lunch. During art therapy I began to feel very agitated and nauseated. Then I felt intensely thirsty, so I was getting a drink every ten minutes. Then my head seemed to be swimming. I told a nurse that I thought I was having a reaction to the increased Desipramine.

July 10 (Wednesday). *I awakened about 3:30 A.M. I feel very nauseated and very thirsty. At 5:00 A.M. I got up for some ginger ale and a cracker. Then I went back to bed and slept for about 45 minutes. . . . I'm trying so hard to believe all of God's promises. I know that they are true and I thank Him that they aren't dependent upon my feeling them. I feel totally hopeless today. I feel that with every day a little more of me dies.*

July 12 (Friday). *I still fear awakening at night and associating that with depression and then getting depressed. When I first get up, I'm somewhat shaky. Dr. King said my blood test showed the Desipramine level was now at 121 mg./ml., so that's still a little low. We played Frisbee golf in the afternoon and I did so terribly I quit and just watched. . . . At 5:45 Tim came to pick me up. We had supper at home and just had a nice evening together. I felt very relaxed and comfortable at home. There were no anxieties. . . . I gave Joel his bedtime bottle and he went down to sleep at 10:00 P.M.*

July 13 (Saturday). *I guess I still have a fear of never feeling normal again. I seem to have a problem with self-confidence. I want to feel like myself and I don't. . . .*

July 14 (Sunday). *I awakened at 4:45 A.M. and asked for a xanax because I felt so nauseated and anxious. I slept about an hour before getting up. One of the nurses asked me if I might be pregnant. I told her I doubted it. I asked for a xanax at around 11:00 A.M. because I am still nauseated and anxious. I went to the chapel service and that was helpful. Reverend Nykamp spoke on trust and anxiety. When I returned I talked with Jackie [a nurse, not her real name] and I felt she implied that I hadn't bonded with Joel and also that I hadn't been*

*pushing myself enough to attend classes. I felt she didn't under-
stand me. I felt very hurt. I called Tim to pick me up at noon.
I told him about my talk with Jackie. He got very angry about
the implication that I hadn't bonded with Joel, especially since
he has been bringing Joel to the hospital regularly so that I can
take care of him. After getting mad myself, I gradually began
to feel a tremendous relief from the depression and the nausea.
The rest of the evening I felt more like my old self than I had
felt in weeks. Joel was awake a long time and I thoroughly
enjoyed him. He fell asleep on my shoulder for an hour. I stayed
home to put Joel to sleep. I returned feeling "I AM GETTING
WELL. I WILL TRUST." I feel so encouraged tonight.*

July 15 (Monday). *I talked with Todd about the incident
with Jackie yesterday. He thought it was good that I verbalized
my anger with Tim over her implications. Maybe that's my
release for anger. Perhaps I should talk with her also. He now
gave me an open pass so I can come and go as I wish. Dr.
King asked me if I wanted my medication increased. I said no
since I was feeling well today. I don't want the nausea back.
I'm really praying for a good week.*

July 18 (Thursday). *I awakened at 4:00 A.M. and went to
get a drink. I could not get back to sleep. I did not feel anxious
then. But around 9:00 A.M. I began to feel nauseated and
became more anxious. In education class I felt so agitated that
I left at 11:3O and came to the ward for a xanax. I couldn't
eat lunch. I attended my afternoon classes but felt very low.
Todd thought most of my depression was gone and it was
anxiety I was dealing with now. I don't feel I understand the
difference. Anxiety is anxiety to me. I went home at 5:45 but
felt extremely tense and shaky. I loved holding Joel and being
with the family but I couldn't calm down. Tim had a ball game
so he brought me back at 7:30. I told the nurses I was feeling
terribly agitated and just couldn't relax. I felt like screaming
and running away to try to run away from myself. I wanted
to die but wouldn't harm myself. I had two xanax an hour*

apart but was hyperventilating and had tingling in my feet and hands. At 9:00 P.M. I began to settle down.

July 19 (Friday). *I awakened at 7:00 A.M. and felt a little dizzy and very sad—not quite depressed or anxious. I think I just feel drugged. Dr. King has increased the Desipramine to 300 mg. He felt the anxiety attack last night was a result of the depression level yet. I felt real good in the afternoon and evening. I thank you Lord for the better day. May all my medication work effectively.*

July 21 (Sunday). *I went home for the weekend. I ate really well this weekend. No nausea. It was wonderful to just be together with the family. I felt like I just wanted to stay home for good—no depression or anxiety. I thank the Lord for this wonderful weekend. I'm praying to go home soon.*

July 22 (Monday). *I feel like my heart is beating real fast when I awaken. When I'm first awake I feel shaky. During group discussion I felt anxiety again, but seemed to keep it under control. I wish I were home. I feel so much more comfortable there. I saw Todd at 1:00 P.M. He said that if I don't have a steady, good week, we will have to switch to some other method of drug therapy next week, a different drug, or ECT. I feel very disappointed.*

July 23 (five weeks). *I feel very anxious when I get up. I'm very shaky. I talked with Jackie and told her I'm scared about ECT and I feel hopeless. My lab report showed my Desipramine level is at 114 mg/ml. That's lower than before. Dr. King asked to talk to me about ECT.*

The first time the letters ECT (electroconvulsant therapy) were mentioned to us, both Pat and I cringed. Pat had received her psychiatric nurse's training during the 1960s, a period when psychiatric therapy was undergoing tremendous changes. Many new drugs were being introduced and what was then called "shock treatment" was being left behind as an outdated and barbaric method of therapy. From the treatments Pat had attended in the sixties, this reaction was probably justified. The seizures were frightening, and the risks to bones and the cardiovascular system quite serious.

The only problem with the rejection of such treatments was the undeniable degree of success they demonstrated. During the 1970s, considerably more study was done and the shock treatment re-emerged as electroconvulsant therapy, a treatment more benign, to be sure, than its predecessor but still one looked forward to with some anxiety. Oddly enough, we welcomed it. The medical treatment to this point had not been successful. We were desperate for alternatives that could be administered quickly and effectively. Still, there were fears. To fully understand this therapy, one has to glimpse back into earlier years of treatment for depression.

Although depression has been recognized as a mental disorder for over two thousand years, treatment of it remained much of a mystery until the twentieth century. As early as 1785, however, convulsions induced by large doses of camphor were used in treating mental disorders, a practice revived in the 1930s for treatment of schizophrenia. In 1938 and 1939 the first safe use of electricity to induce convulsions was developed.

With the safer gauges of the convulsion by use of electroencepholograms, the entire procedure acquired greater clarity during the late fifties and early sixties. Essentially, the application of a current through two electrodes placed on the forehead produced a grand mal seizure, two effects of which were a marked stimulation of cerebral circulation and an increase of hormonal activity in the brain, particularly of the neurohormone serotonin.

Dr. John White, a Christian psychiatrist who has used ECT in his practice, points out in *The Masks of Melancholy* that "it is unfortunate that negative findings about ECT receive more publicity than careful studies about its true value."[31] Arguing from several case studies, Dr. White asserts that ECT is an effective and valuable treatment under proper conditions and upon proper patients. The benefits, he points out, "have nothing to do with electricity nor with the methods by which convulsions are produced. The biological consequences of convulsions (a release of neurotransmitters) lead to the improvement. The longer each convulsion lasts, the more pronounced is the curative effect of ECT."[32]

In recent years the procedure has been modified substantially, chiefly through the use of muscle relaxant drugs to ease the effects of the seizure. In her *Clinical Handbook of Depression,* Janice Wood Wetzel describes preparations for this procedure:

> Subjects are not allowed to eat or drink for at least four hours prior to treatment. Tranquilizers or sedatives may be used to reduce fear and/or resistance. Atropine, a common preanesthetic medication, is administered half an hour in advance in order to dry secretions in the mouth and airway, thus reducing the risk of suffocation and any complications that might result from swallowing saliva. Dentures, sharp jewelry, and hairpins are removed; bowels and bladders are emptied, and the patient is ready for treatment.[33]

The patient is then placed on a padded table and a graphite jelly is rubbed onto the temples where the electrodes will be placed. The jelly prevents burns and increases conductivity of the electricity. After placing a rubber gag in the mouth to protect the teeth and tongue during the administration, the doctor injects the patient with a fast-action barbiturate that puts the patient asleep. A muscle relaxant is also injected to protect against broken bones or back injuries. Wetzel further describes the actual administration:

> The electrodes are placed at the temples. Seventy to 175 volts of electricity penetrate the brain for one-tenth of one and one half seconds. Almost immediately the facial muscles stiffen, indicating that the tonic phase of the convulsion has begun. The clonic, or active, phase starts in ten seconds and continues for thirty to forty seconds. The modified procedure causes a slight twitching in the toes, immeasurable improvement over the grand mal seizures that result when a preventive muscle relaxant has not been administered.[34]

ECT, although demonstrated as effective against depression (studies since the 1940s have indicated short- and long-term relief comparing as favorably or more favorably than pharmaceutical treatment), is still attended by many objections. Although the newer, more benign treatment described above has avoided some of the more serious side effects such as broken bones or cardiac arrest found in earlier treatments, other side effects are still pronounced. The primary of these is headache. With medication, Pat usually found relief from the headache within twenty-four hours.

A second demonstrated side effect is short-term memory loss, lasting sometimes for several days. Following a treatment, Pat would have little recollection of events immediately preceding or following the treatment. She would have difficulty remembering names or focusing her thoughts. Sometimes she would have difficulty remembering events of days, weeks, or even months prior. Dates, events, and people would be confused in sequences. Although some critics of ECT claim there is irretrievable memory loss, studies indicate otherwise. Many ECT treatments today are unilateral; that is, the electrodes are placed on the right side of the brain, the nonverbal hemisphere, to reduce memory loss.

Other people object that ECT is a dehumanizing course of treatment. The depressed person, already suffering from an intolerable sense of unworthiness, is further degraded by being strapped to a table and charged with electricity. Moreover, it can be perceived by the patient as a kind of justified punishment for failures. I believe these objections have little merit. If the procedure is carefully explained to the patient, if the patient is carefully attended through the procedure—both of which were the case with Pat—there should be no such feelings. It is simply one additional and effective course of treatment for depression. It should seldom be the first course of treatment, but has its legitimate place when properly administered during proper intervals.

Despite some reservations in the medical world, the modern, carefully controlled procedure of ECT has demonstrated clear success. Although it was a second course of treatment with Pat, due to her inability to effectively metabolize the antidepressant drug, some psychiatrists are arguing that it ought to be an earlier treatment. Dr. White assesses the treatment in relation to antidepressants:

> The debate about the superiority of ECT over antidepressant drugs continues. Slowly we are coming to realize that ECT is faster and somewhat safer than antidepressants. It is more effective in women than in men. Memory impairment and headaches remain disadvantages, especially when the electrodes are placed on both sides of the head. It is not without risk, even risk to life, though the task force appointed by the American Psychiatric Association found that death occurred

'extremely rarely.' Indeed ECT is much safer either than leaving the depression untreated or than treating depression with tricyclic antidepressants.[35]

While such comparative issues remain hotly debated, we can say in confidence that ECT is certainly not comparable to the old-fashioned "shock treatments," and that it is not necessarily a procedure to be feared in treatment of depression.

One unexpected side effect did bother Pat. ECT will induce some short-term sluggishness (the patient will often sleep for a few hours following treatment) and some numbness. As is indicated in the journal entries, Pat experienced acute tingling and numbness in her extremities. Since she had had meningitis six years prior, the doctors saw this as a caution that the treatments should stop. However, they had proven so successful in relieving her depression that it was unlikely the course would have gone much further anyway. While the normal course of treatments is six to twelve, some patients find relief with as few as one.

In Pat's case, this initially feared procedure became the cruel mercy that posed the first dramatic breakthrough in six weeks.

July 23 (Tuesday). Five weeks. My lab report showed my Desipramine level is at 114 mg/ml. That's lower than before. Dr. King asked to talk to me about ECT. I agreed to start tomorrow. I had to have a consultation with Dr. Christenson also. He will give me the first five treatments. I'm very anxious and apprehensive today. I attended most of my classes though. I also had to have an EKG. Sometimes I feel a sense of peace coming over me. I thank God for that. I took a sleeping pill.

July 24 (Wednesday). I got up at 6:45 to shower. At 7:45 an aide walked me over to the Van Noord building for my first

ECT. *I don't remember anything after being put to sleep and getting back to my room. I have a headache. I took Tylenol at 9:00 A.M. I rested a while and then went to an appointment with Todd at 11:00 A.M. That was hard because I was so extremely tired and confused and didn't feel I could think clearly. So I left after 15 minutes. I ate a little lunch and took more Tylenol at 1:00 P.M. During class at 1:00 P.M., I was so tired I could hardly stay awake. I came back to the room and slept from 2-4:00. Then I called Tim and he came for me with Joel. I love my precious family and thank God for a peaceful feeling today.*

July 25 (Thursday). Many patients have asked me about ECT. My appetite is good today. I don't seem to feel depressed.

July 26 (Friday). I awakened at 5:00 A.M. I dozed until I got up at 7:00, but was very anxious waiting for my ECT at 9:00 A.M., so I walked the mile to the center. I was tearful before the ECT that they wouldn't help relieve the depression. Dr. Christenson said that was just the depression telling me that. I had a hard time awakening from the ECT. I kept wanting to sleep. I have a horrible headache.

July 29 (Monday). I had my third ECT today. I asked Dr. Christenson if this could be my last one. He said I would have to talk to my doctor. I was very nauseated after this ECT. Extra strength Tylenol given for a headache. I have a distant, confused feeling in my head. At my appointment with Todd, I talked about being discharged. I want to leave this week but he said that I need more treatments. He said we can work for next week.

July 31 (Wednesday). It's a rainy, cool morning. Today was my fourth ECT. I'm nauseated and dizzy after it. I took Tylenol for a headache. I have a strange sensation in my arms and legs after this ECT—like they are dead weights or like the muscles are going to collapse completely. I didn't go to any morning classes. In the afternoon I still feel weak. I want so much to go home because I get so homesick for the family, but tonight being discharged seems a little overwhelming.

August 1 (Thursday). I still have the feeling of heaviness in my arms and legs. I think it's from the muscle relaxant, Anectine.

August 4 (Sunday). I feel the weekend has gone great, much better than I dared anticipate. I come back with the feeling that I'm putting in my last week here.

August 5 (Monday). I only slept until about 5:30 A.M., so had only four hours of sleep last night. I just feel very excited about being discharged. I am real restless in my morning classes. I can hardly wait for my 1:00 P.M. appointment with Todd to tell him how well the weekend went. I am so excited when I see him. He says I may be discharged tomorrow after Tim and I come in for an appointment. I ran to the phone to tell Tim. I skipped my afternoon classes except for spiritual growth. I saw Dr. King and Dr. Van Eerden at 4:30 P.M. The dosage of Desipramine was reduced to 200 mg. because of the heaviness of muscles which I felt in my arms and legs after the last ECT.

August 6 (Tuesday). I slept about four-and-a-half hours last night. Tim came at 9:30 for a joint appointment with Todd. He reminds us that I must recover slowly, not try to be "super-mom" right away. I feel confident it will work out at home.

I understood the feeling Pat had as we drove away from the hospital toward home. I too had felt it once. Driving home from the hospital that day, that Tuesday in August while the summer sun shone in the trees, and life for so many went its accustomed way, my mind flashed back again to another day . . .

It was 114 degrees at the air base at Long Binh, Vietnam. I stood in a long line, jungle fatigues drenched with sweat, waiting with other men to board an airplane. Behind us lay months of worry and agony. No one in that line spoke. We stood there quietly, shuffling, nervous, while the sun beat down on our sweaty, gaunt bodies. We still had the red muck of the Delta caked on our jungle boots; fatigues hung like limp rags from our bodies. But I remember the silence. No one spoke.

When we climbed the ramp a few men smiled. We fell into the seats and buckled the seatbelts. In the aisle ahead a man bent and mumbled a prayer. Tears were on his sun-whipped cheeks. Other than that there was silence. The engines began to whine. The great ship taxied to the end of the runway. We waited while a trio of Phantom jet fighters roared off the runway, their huge engines belching a plume of black smoke. And it struck us for a moment: they were flying away from us. Still, no one spoke.

The engines' whine rose to a scream. The great bird bucked on its brakes against the massive thrust. A voice told us to check our seatbelts. No one moved. No one spoke.

With the brake release and the sudden thrust, a huge expulsion of breath, a communal sigh of over two hundred men, sounded through the plane. Still no one spoke. The craft roared down the runway like a great, awkward animal, eating asphalt, belching exhaust, roaring now—the scream of engines an anguished cry. The nose tilted. The thrust socked us back in our seats. The plane achieved flight. The dark line of the jungle dipped below one window. Dipped, and began to disappear. Not the long hover over its dark spaces which I had seen over and over again from the helicopters I flew in. No, the dip and disappearance and the screaming roar upward and the turn not in but out to the coast and the ocean's vast expanse and the world that lay beyond. And two hundred men cried and shouted and laughed.

And on this August morning I knew what Pat felt.

8 On Dry Land: Rediscovering Home Patterns

W e who are well tend to believe that a person's health is signified by hospital discharge, when in fact the road to health has just been started. The return home, in any illness, is a fragile and vulnerable period.

If one has suffered from depression, this return, this traveling on the road back to health, is especially vulnerable. It is not the case alone for the hospitalized patient, but also for the patient on the road back from therapy or outpatient treatment. It is the case for anyone who has been depressed and now is trying to establish a new order. Since our particular situation involved a lengthy hospitalization and separation from the family, we will focus primarily on that event that was firsthand to us, that pattern we came to know best. However, the lessons we learned apply to others who have suffered depression; indeed, they apply to those who have suffered any serious illness.

We want to consider some of the stages back to health—they are stages, not sudden developments but a relearning of patterns that accompany the way back from depression. We can speak only from experience here, for there is little published and few case study materials on the subject. Again, the assumption for the hospitalized patient is that discharge signals health; and for the outpatient, that an end to therapy signals an end to the effects of the illness or problem. Actually those points only signal a new beginning. What guidelines might assist that new beginning?

First—in order and importance—*the person has to relearn the patterns, the rhythms, of living.* The difficulty with this effort lies in the fact that the person has changed by virtue of the illness. Depression will make us see things differently, think about things differently, do things differently, and feel things differently. We have to accept the fact that our lives have changed. The tension lies in the other fact of equal significance—that we want things to be just the same as always. We want to establish common patterns that we remember as normal and affirming.

In our situation the experience developed like this. First of all, I had been the primary nurturer of the family for seven weeks. I was the authority not just for big decisions but for all those daily routines that keep the family gears running in order. This was especially true, of course, of care for the baby. A fourteen-week-old baby is quite different from a seven- week-old baby. However much I tried to involve Pat in child care during her hospitalization, and to keep her in close contact with baby Joel, he was a different baby than he had been. He had had different illnesses, different sleeping patterns, different foods.

The very first thing the depressed person has to recognize— and it is an admission also to a new way of living— is these differences. I also had to confess that things would be different with Pat back home. This was no less difficult an acceptance for me. For weeks my schedule had been tied, not to my work, but to the action of home. I confronted the hard realization that I had to *give up* so that Pat could *come back*.

I can't say that we thought this through in a logical, contractual way, neatly dividing responsibilities. Rather, it was a case of being acutely sensitive to each other's needs and possible pressure points. Suddenly Pat was asking me questions about care for the baby that I had simply assumed because I had been *doing* those answers twenty-four hours a day. The shock of recognition was this: They were the very questions I might have asked seven weeks prior. How much cereal does he eat for breakfast? How long does Joel nap? Does he still get his medicine? How much? These vitamins? And so on.

And the questions extended to the other children. Has Jeff heard about his class schedule yet? Do the children need school clothes? Books? Folders? Knapsacks?

These are not responsibilities one can contract, yet families must remain sensitive to the needs of each other, recognizing the subtle interplay of desires and abilities. Pat needed to re-establish her role in our home as primary nurturer. I needed to sense those areas in which she needed support and assistance to do this. Moreover, it had to be done gradually as the steps that confirmed that role became more firm. The second lesson arises as a caution also. It may be phrased as *the compulsion to succeed*. To succeed, the person will often try to do too much. Herein lies a danger, and one can readily see the link with our first point. Having been ill, the person longs for wellness. Having been apart from family routines, the person wants to take up those routines that are associated with wellness. But, that person also wants to get well, feel well, as quickly as possible. If I work as hard as possible, so the thinking goes, I will feel well more quickly.

We noted in the previous chapter that Pat's therapist warned her not to try to be "supermom." Indeed. The person getting well has to adjust goals to meet abilities. Those abilities are not the same as before the illness.

Because of this link between the depressed person's goals and the association of certain previous patterns with being well, the psychological reaction might go one of two ways. The first reaction might be a pronounced apathy about household routines and goals. Believing herself not to be fully well yet, and believing herself to be different from other "normal" people, she might re-engage normal routines with a decided lack of engagement. That isn't just fancy double talk, but a psychological reality. Because the person feels unable to succeed at routine tasks, and fears failure, the person simply refuses to assume normal duties.

This might be evidenced by a long period of social withdrawal, an unwillingness to return to work, or an inability to work hard and systematically. He or she might take little interest in household matters, leaving the spouse to run those routines. In certain cases, medication might be partly responsible for this lethargy. There may be a fear of meeting other people because they might remind the person that he has been ill, or because they might induce stress. The person remains unwilling to make decisions. In short, the symptoms of the depression become habitual.

On the other hand, the reaction to this link between the depressed person's goals and the association of certain previous patterns with being well might induce an almost frantic effort to succeed. The person wants so desperately to re-assume the routine that he or she believes it can be achieved by hard work alone.

I felt a certain helplessness when it occurred to us. Here was the tension. First, I had been primary nurturer and felt awkward and threatened relinquishing that task.

Second, the therapist had cautioned us specifically against Pat's trying to do too much at first. Therefore, I felt I should be slow to relinquish my tasks. Third, Pat was eager to work her way back into routines and her normal role. The tensions developed and resolved themselves in an odd fashion.

I thought I had kept a decently clean house during those weeks. True, I didn't bother with cobwebs along the ceiling. True, the kitchen became a repository for toys—so convenient to drop them off there when we came in the back door. And I didn't know that it's a good idea to move the furniture once in a while when you vacuum. It never dawned on me. I covered up nicely. We have gardens all around our house and all summer long I have bouquets of fresh cut flowers and roses placed around the house. A good way to divert attention.

I must confess there was a lot of dirt I didn't see. Cleanliness is relative after all. Nobody in our family would dream of disturbing my study. I know exactly where things are, what piles of papers contain what writings. It seems neat to me, as long as I can find things without too much hunting. And I'm the only one who has to live there. Four or five times a year I enter with a vacuum and dust rags and rearrange those piles. Yet, I faintly understood that the rest of the house also belonged to the family and that a greater degree of apparent order had to prevail there.

Although she has never been a compulsive housecleaner, Pat quietly but deliberately set about cleaning the day after she got home. Actually, the wonder was that she waited so long. She scrubbed floors, moved furniture, pushed the vacuum over places I didn't know existed. I thought the underside of the sofa was there to stick books in when you finished reading them. She pulled out a stack of books a foot high, half of them overdue library books. And so it went.

Cautiously I reminded her of the therapist's words. "Take it easy," I cautioned. She threw me a look of exasperation. "I want to do this," she said. But you can sense the effect: I began to feel that *I* had failed. Granted, I'm a lousy housekeeper. But I had tried. Pat assured me I had done a wonderful job—as she got a clean bucket of scrub water. I found something else to do for the day, something besides cleaning my study.

A certain degree of control was passing from one set of hands to another. It was a necessary passing, but also a delicate one as the old rhythms of the home were established.

Such experiences as these might mark any marital relationship for any number of reasons. A good marriage will be marked by assumption of responsibilities in certain areas and by a clear understanding of differing areas of authority. Such understandings are seldom present from the day of the marriage onward, or drawn up clearly like a set of legal obligations. Rather they are the fruit of years of getting to know each other's strong and weak points. They are marks of a good marriage that must be relearned after a separation and a confusion of domestic roles.

The heart of the return to normalcy for a depressed person, however, lies not in external events but *in the rediscovery of selfhood*. Studies of depression have left many loopholes and unanswered questions. One is this matter of finding one's way back to health. To understand it, remember some of the key symptoms of depression. Afflicted with the illness, the person's self-image diminishes to the point of nonexistence. The concept of self-worth crumbles like ashes. Personality, that sense of and expression of who we are, seems impossibly impeded by a gray cloud of anxiety and presumed unworthiness.

Because of the acute sense of loss of selfhood, the

experience of depression has frequently been compared with the stages of grief in the experience of a loved one's death. The parallel can be seen if we compare the four traditional stages commonly associated with grief with the experience of depression.

First: *Denial*. In the first stage of grief, one refuses to acknowledge the loss, and wants the person back. One longs for the customary order of former relationships. Early stages of depression are almost always marked by denial of the symptoms and the illness. "This can't be happening to me" is, perhaps, the most common sentiment. But the denial moves beyond that to the loss of personhood that accompanies the illness. In early stages, the depressed person keeps telling himself, "I'll snap back. If I can hold out a little longer I'll be my old self."

Second: *Anger*. In grief, the person will become angry as he senses the reality of the loss. This anger turns in several directions: at himself for things he might have done better in relation to the dead person, at God for allowing the loss, and even at the deceased person for dying and leaving the grieving person with these feelings. Similarly, depressed persons will often feel anger at themselves for feeling this way, at God for allowing it to happen, at others for either "causing" the depression or for not being depressed themselves. The "aloneness" of the depressed person is accentuated in this stage.

Third: *Despair*. In the grief experience this stage is often called "depression" since it involves feelings of hopelessness and intense sadness. The grieving person believes that life is worthless without the loved one, that there is no reason to go on living without him. The comparable stage in depression is the acute sense of helplessness and alienation from life. Life in its present state holds no meaning or value, and there appears to be no future hope. The depressed person may wish that he were dead at this stage, the nadir of the illness.

Fourth: *Acceptance.* In grief the person must, by himself and with the aid of others, understand that the loved one has died and that life must go on in new ways. Acceptance is not denial; rather, it is finding a new way to *live with the loss.* In depression, the person must also confront the inseparability of the illness from his own life story. By knowing the illness, the depressed person can begin, with the aid of others, to understand how to live with it. In time it will take a background place in life. This last stage involves the matter of re-inventing a life, one that now includes the experience of depression.

The act of coming home from depression, of emerging from its cruel sea, is also at once an act of rediscovery. One must relearn one's self, perhaps even re-invent one's self. Understand also that the depression, which may take as long as eighteen months to leave the body (that is, for the biochemical system to attain full stability), will not fully leave the person alone to an easy adjustment. The depressed person on the way to recovery is both *fighting for* a renewed self and *fighting against* the affliction of selflessness. The struggle is a difficult one at a fragile time. It may be helpful to consider the struggle in terms of rewriting one's own personal story, one that now includes suffering. The person must find a place for that in the story. Since depression rips from a person a sense of selfhood—the sense of acting significantly in a life story—the person on the way back is rediscovering a past, identifying a present, and redefining a future all at once. Essentially, the person re-invents himself as the central character in his own story.

One of the few essays that discusses this phenomenon of emerging from depression appears in *American Behavioral Scientist.* In "Emerging from Depression," Ernest Keen describes the formidable tasks of his own emergence. He accurately describes what he emerges from—a necessary first step. One must know the starting point for any story. Here are Keen's words:

> Depression is experienced as the stoppage of time, the emptiness of space. . . . Time stops; development of myself, of situations, and of relationships all grind to a halt. Everything appears static, dead, with no change except a progressive deterioration like rusting or rotting. Most of all, the future ceases being really future, really new, unknown, fruitful. Rather, the future seems to promise only a dreary repetition of the past. Space is empty. There are things, but they have lost their importance. My house, once a haven and a home, is a mere building, drained of its echoes of vitality and love. My clothes, once full of interest for me, now hang gaping stupidly in my closet. . . .
>
> Depression runs counter not only to rationality, as symptoms do. It also runs counter to and violates the *elan* of life itself, that vital force that lies so deep in our being that we never notice it until it is absent, as in death, or blocked and negated, as in depression.
>
> The giving up of depression is saying, simply, "I can't"—a feeling of hopelessness and helplessness. Adjacent to "I can't" are "I won't," which is angry, and "I shouldn't," which is guilty. All these yield paralysis, but the anger and the guilt are agitated; they have not yet given up.[36]

Because depression strips one of a sense of selfhood and robs one of a sense of past and future, Keen points out that we have to re-invent ourselves in emerging from depression:

> My present life, which leads from the past into the future, matters when it is part of a historical unfolding within which I can place

> myself in an integral part. . . . In depression,
> these ordinary aspects of life have been neu-
> tralized—rendered   meaningless—by   the
> death themes of depression: the stoppage of
> time, the emptiness of space, and the deifica-
> tion of people. The re-establishment of a fu-
> ture, the refurnishing of space with signifi-
> cance and vitality, and the repersonification
> of others are all implicated in reinventing my-
> self and emerging from depression.[37]

To fulfill this, Keen points out, one begins in an act of
faith, a sense of desire and willingness to rebuild.

Risks attend this act of faith which is the emergence
from depression, as they attend all actions of faith. Søren
Kierkegaard once wrote that faith is a matter of "fear
and trembling." The depressed person, rediscovering
himself, understands this. But that act of faith—of affirming a future and self-worth—is guided, writes Keen, by
beginning to trust others and relationships. It is also
guided by a firmness of belief and an unwillingness to
give in to quick cures.

Accepting these premises, it may be said nonetheless
that one never fully emerges from depression. It is now
a part of one's past, and has influenced one's present
and future hope. This cannot be denied. In the time
since her hospitalization Pat has twice, under medical
supervision, gone off her medication and has had to
resume it both times. The first time, a year after her
hospitalization, she went without medication for several
months. At first things went very well. She could exercise
again. She loved the feeling of being free from any medication. Then, subtly at first, the depression which had
not fully left her began to insinuate its poison.

It happened like this. As her feelings became increasingly sad, her depression told her she had always felt
like this and always would. Her rational mind shouted

back: *No! This is not me! Depression is a deceit, a lie to personhood.* Depression almost got the upper hand before she started on the medication again.

The second time she tried to reduce her medication for only a week. At the first signs of depression she started back at her regular maintenance dosage. This time she fought back immediately, denying the lie of the illness. And that was a victory. She has rediscovered herself, found a new story. To be sure, she wishes that it were a story free of depression. She wishes mightily that she would not have to rely on an antidepressant at all, and looks forward to the time when she will be free from it. But if that is part of the story—at this page, this chapter—she has determined also to see it through, not to flip ahead too quickly so that the pages are lost.

That is the temptation—to try to do it too quickly. People want to deny the reality of the experience of depression and to eradicate the bad memory of it. It can't be done. It is a part of the person who has suffered from it, a page in that person's story. To obliterate it is also to obliterate, once again, what it means now to be that person. The challenge of emergence from depression is actually two-fold: to understand that it is indeed a real chapter in the story of your life and to understand that it is by no means the final chapter.

The story does go on. There may be uneven stretches. But as Scripture authoritatively promises us, the Christian story can have *only one ending*: the huge joy that lies beyond human conception in the eternal story which has no room, no pages at all, for sorrow and suffering.

"He will wipe away every tear from their eyes. . . ." (Revelation 21:4).

9   Compass Points:
Understanding Suffering

W hy is it that when one feels compelled to write about suffering the words become either pinched and narrow or they become broad and sprawling? One wants to write either a poem, compressing it all inward, or a novel, letting it sprawl into vastness. Suffering refuses precision. We know it by experience, not first of all by rational argument, neat discussion, or precise categories.

We know it when it happens to us, those times when prayers pant at the lips or achieve only half-formed words in the pleading mind. We know it when we sit with others on the mourner's bench, girded in grief. We seldom know it by calculated argument or honeyed words. They spin around the periphery of our suffering and fail to knive to the heart clad in sorrow.

At such times, when we feel the fiery torment of suffering, we tend to look to others for solace, for comfort, for answers. We want patterns more than answers. We want to know who survived, and how, and why? Why?

Yes, because there are those moments so steeped in suffering that we utter only *why?*, and it means so many unanswerable things. Why does this happen, Lord? And why to me, Lord? And why should I keep on living at all, Lord? The plaintive *why*, perhaps the most tortured word in our vocabulary, and the first word in the vocabulary of those who suffer.

Theology provides us answers. Suffering, we are told, is inescapable in this fallen world. Once having allowed the taint of sin to enter, humanity is stained by it. Satan has a hold on this world; the claws of the raging lion cut deeply and are not easily released. And so we suffer. We are at the mercy of our fallen condition. To be sure, Jesus has won the victory. We know that the stain is washed whiter than snow. We know the lion has limits cast upon him by the almighty power of God and by the victory of the cross. We know that God works miracles to thwart, defeat, overcome, and turn aside the raging lion. The *Heidelberg Cathechism* tells us that "God will avert all evil, or turn it to your profit," and we accept with our rational understanding that this is true. And we know that the day is coming when the resurrection power of the risen Lord will smash, with unendurable brilliance, the power of the beast of darkness, and that believers will revel in a new kingdom of light where there is no more darkness, nor crying, nor suffering. We know this even while we suffer in the state of fallenness. Theology tells us this; we know this to be true.

Still the tortured first word of the suffering, those who have not yet had the evil averted or turned to profit, echoes: *Why?*

Pastoral counseling provides us answers. Here theology turns from concept to precept, from words to living. And so pastoral counseling tells us that the suffering are being tested, so that they may be found firm, so that they may be stronger for having suffered, so that they may model a way for others. Pastoral counseling points us to 2 Corinthians 1:3-4: "Blessed be the God and Father of our Lord Jesus Christ, the Father of mercies and God of all comfort, who comforts us in all our affliction, so that we may be able to comfort those who are in any affliction, with the comfort with which we ourselves are comforted by God." We know this also to be true. The saints of the ages stand before us in mute testimony and exhortation. The stoned Stephen casts his eyes heavenward, and we should do the same. The martyr braves the lions in the coliseum or the fire at the stake, and submits to the terror of the way to affirm a way for others. And we should do the same, mindful that we are always modeling Jesus to the eyes of the world.

Yet that terrible first word in the vocabulary of the suffering, those who don't feel the comfort at *this* time, lingers: *Why?*

Ethics tells us that we must live in neighbor love, and that by suffering ourselves we learn to sympathize with and actively engage in the sufferings of others. We are afflicted to open our eyes to the needs of a suffering world, to turn our vision from things of this world to the needs of this world. We suffer in order to be mindful of others huddled in the cloak of suffering. We know this also to be true. Too often we place our love in the possession of things; too often we become slaves to them. Nikolai Berdyaev wrote in *Slavery and Freedom* that "The slavery of man increases in proportion to the growth of materiality." Surely one means of freedom from such slavery is to be stripped of our attachment to things, from the tyranny of possessions, through suffering. And, yes, we know the huge affliction of this world—the bloated abdomens of the starving millions, the bodies huddled over steam grates in the inner cities, the hovels of fear that some call a home. We know this to be true, and our hearts and minds and the works of our hands and dollars turn to them.

But the word, *that* word, scrapes rawly across our lips: *Why?*

Medical science, or the interpreters of medical science try too often to objectify suffering into statistics. They might tell us that pain is a necessary biological phenomenon. Indeed, we ought to be grateful for it. Consider a world without pain. The cut on your finger, untended because unnoticed, would fester with infection and endanger the hand itself. The pain along the right side of the abdomen, if not present, would not provide someone the signal of the impending rupture of an appendix. The headaches that might signal a tumor, the pain of decaying teeth—all these pains are essential to our health. We could not live in a world without pain. The tragedy of leprosy is precisely the evacuation of pain; the deadly effects in the truncated limbs and festering sores bear evidence. By analogy, then, the pain of stress makes one mindful of the need for healing; the pain of depression makes one mindful of the need for therapy. We have these pains, this suffering, to become well again.

But why, *why*, can't I be well without the suffering?

Psychology, too, has entered the fray of rational responses to the experience of suffering. We suffer to become more aware of ourselves and to become better persons for that awareness. Thus, Tim Stafford says, in *Knowing the Face of God,*

> Suffering is lonely, and its most obvious effect is to bring the sufferer into a new relationship with himself. Suffering does not teach from a textbook; it works with the material, cutting away layer after soft layer until only firmer stuff remains. All the dross goes: the ambitions, love of money, vanity about appearance, everything that sets us above others in

> our own mind. Suffering purges everything
> that is not central to life.[38]

Truly, suffering turns us inward. But the political prisoner in the Soviet gulag, stripped of everything except his person; the cancer victim in the throes of radiation, stripped of everything except a tenuous balance between life and death; the grieving, the depressed, and the lonely wonder why this "person" cannot be nurtured in better ways than by suffering.

Some religions might say that one suffers because of a committed sin. Sin is defilement; it does cause suffering. The suffering, then, signals the need for identification and exorcism of that sin. True, we know that sin causes suffering. We know also that sin, even when forgiven, bears consequences. Christians cannot be so naive as to deny this. Neither can Christians take upon themselves their own forgiveness. This Jesus has done. Once and for all. In him, our sins are buried in the deepest sea. In him, we need no agent other than our prayer for forgiveness and his limitless grace to forgive. We know—this we believe, this we cherish—that *all* our sins are forgiven in Jesus.

But, *Why*, then? Why do I suffer?

To be sure, there are other questions and answers about suffering; promptings of the rational mind, not the suffering spirit. One person asks, "Aren't we to praise God for all things and at all times?" This person believes we are to praise God for and in suffering. We can indeed praise God as the Lord of life, but not for evil. God is not Satan. God indeed permits Satan a degree of latitude in this fallen world, but God hates that evil and has promised an end to it and a new world free from evil. Never should we confuse the dark signs of our fallenness with the bright goodness of God. Jesus himself didn't praise God for his suffering, but pleaded for its removal, nonetheless submitting to the will of God. We may, as 1 Thessalonians 5:18 tells us, praise God *in* suffering, but not *for* suffering.

Truly, Pat and I affirmed things we already believed through this suffering we endured. These were truths brought home to us in new ways.

We affirmed, and cherish, the preciousness of each individual life. How marvelously and fearfully each of us is made. We emerged from the sea of suffering willing that no one, not one single person, be forsaken to its brutal tide. We understand also that each individual is unique, possessing individual hopes, dreams, failures, pressure points. Never again will we look at people as masses; we look at them as individual creations of God.

We affirmed, furthermore, that each person, sooner or later, bears a cross of suffering. We have learned to look past faces and appearances and discern the heart. I am particularly mindful of this in my profession of teaching. Too often I used to look upon students in a class; now I see that class comprised of individuals with individual needs. This need for discernment struck me dramatically some time ago. A student commented on her terrible loneliness. She would actually go into her dormitory bathroom and turn on the shower so that her crying wouldn't disturb her roommates. Her final comment haunts me: "I just wanted someone to walk to the coffee shop with me." Never again will Pat and I see a person by an appearance, but will see the person behind the appearance.

We affirmed that we need others to care for us, that God works through humans to provide deeds of mercy and lovingkindness. We learned how desperately we need others to lift us up and the huge responsibility we have to be loving and kind—those old, hard words—to others.

We affirmed, surprisingly, the brevity of this life, that

this life is not the end of the Christian way of living—or the non-Christian way of living. I say "surprisingly" because we affirmed this when each day seemed too long and the hours toward health hung like weights. But time itself affirmed that time as we know it will one day end. Our longing for rejoicing pointed us to a day of rejoicing beyond time. Our horror of affliction undeniably reminded us of the horror of suffering that will attend that final separation from God we call hell. How urgent the Christian task to point others the way toward spiritual rejoicing.

These things we affirmed, lessons through suffering, yet they helped us but little to understand why we suffer. The answers tumble before the whimper of the first and last word in the vocabulary of the sufferer.

Having suffered, we are less quick to offer quick answers. Instead, we want to do something: to hold the suffering in our arms. We only wish that we had arms large enough to hold them all. At least we can point the way in which it might be done. For this is the only, the one and only, sufficient answer we have found in suffering. To point to one whose arms open wide enough to embrace a stricken world. The only answer we can find is to point the sufferer to the cross, not to answer the *why*, but to give in its place the overwhelming solace of *because*.

Because Jesus lives, we have a reason for living. Because he loves us. Because he suffered for us and having suffered has entered into our suffering with us. In suffering, one needs not answers, but love. That is the only sufficient answer we can find. It lies in the answer to all of life's paralyzing riddles: the love of Jesus.

That answer was slow in coming to us. There were hints along the way, to be sure. At the moment of her bleakest despair, Pat turned to me once and said, "I couldn't go on living if it weren't for Jesus." Amen, dear friend. Amen. But I am mindful of the fact that she voiced this great "I Believe" at the very moment when she felt the answers the least. Not until some time later could she affirm in feeling what she had voiced in words.

Many months later this lesson in faith came home to us once and for all, with that solidity of conviction that knows no denial. Again, it came through suffering. Suffering is the crooked road of life; and its only roadsign is faith. Here, months later, we faced the turn in the road that confirmed the way. Here, on the narrow way.

How could I deny this simple request? We stood there in a room grown suddenly cold, gathered around the one who was oblivious to our discussion, whose ears were tuned to sounds rather than words. She understood the whistle which meant "come here," and she came. Short, crooked legs beat the sidewalk in her hurry. She understood other sounds: "Go in the kitchen." "Get out of the garden." "Time for a walk."

She did not understand these words—words agonized over, now coldly intractable when uttered. They were words for human understanding, not for this dog.

And when those words that meant she would die were uttered, along with urgent explanations, through tears, I was left with this request of yours, Tamara, which so confounded me: "May I be the last one to kiss Lasha goodbye?" How does a father deny his child's plea?

This was a hard and different thing from those that had gone before. The goldfish, for example, which we dumped down the drain pipe at the park. They would find rivers somewhere. The turtle, for example, which we carried to the creek and watched hunker its plodding way, horny beak eager, to the water's edge. Or like the hamster which staggered around its cage for a week, needing death like a benediction to the miles it had run in its glass cage. Needing the blessing of the cold earth on a Thanksgiving morning as I took it out to the garden—alone, before the children awakened. When I raised the shovel to strike the blow, the hamster fixed me with a glassy, dark eye. I held there for a moment, the eye a mirror in which I suddenly saw myself, old and helpless and begging and fearful, before the shovel fell.

No, this was different by far. This was a part of ourselves, an excision of life by the cruel cautery of conflicting loves. That is why your wish was so hard to grant, so confounding. "May I be the last to kiss Lasha goodbye?" Can you understand this, my daughter Tamara; your profound love was the thing that broke my heart, that causes my own tears in quiet hours.

It would have been so much easier to deny that love, to give the old lie—it's only a dog, after all.

This dog Lasha, this floppy-eared, stubby-legged, wooly-haired dog Lasha, was a member of the family. We bought her as a family venture, each child, along with Mom and Dad, chipping in for her cost. Technically, she was a Lhasa Apso, the heroic, Tibetan "Lion Dog." During her seven years, the only would-be burglar she ever scared away, that I know of, was my brother when he dropped off two dozen eggs on his way to work at 5:00 A.M. one morning. Nonetheless, she defended the house against threats real and imaginary with a ferocity that belied her size.

That became part of the problem. A sedate, regal dog, one obviously unaware of her comically undershot jaw and diminutive stature, she was a warrior at heart. Quick, in her later years too quick, to nip a danger in the bud. Each of the three older children bore wounds as evidence at one time or another. These wounds seemed only to deepen their love for this lion dog, this dustmop, this wobbly paunch of hair and jaw.

We called her "Lasha," a pejoration of her regal title, a domestication of the lineage. We called her that among other things: "Rug!" "Carpet!" "Dustmop!" and Tammy's favorite, "Lasha P. Dog." To all of them she responded with unperturbed affection. Those nips came in unguarded moments, when someone disturbed her nap, for example, and suddenly the old lineage that coursed undeniably in her veins broke loose. Affectionate she was, this dog. What the authoritative books describe as "bright, intelligent eyes" were hidden under a mop of blond hair, like a shaggy wig with comical teeth protruding from it, the whole of which she had a way of nuzzling into a loose hand to beg a scratch.

Sometimes I feel the loss of her when I get up in the morning, even after a year's absence, and fail to hear those paws clattering across the kitchen linoleum. I feel it when I go out for a walk and have to stop the whistle that comes to my lips calling her to join me. I feel it at night when I sit in the chair and my hand dangles loose, the fingers limp with no nuzzling force to fit them. And I wonder what my daughter feels: Tamara who was the last to kiss her goodbye.

It came about like this. There were the three children and the dog. Then the unexpected fourth and the dog. And the fourth was as rambunctious as Lasha was skittish. Here we arrive at definitions. Here we confront the crooked road where words don't seem to fit right, but where sounds have to carry meaning and become words. One was a child; the other a dog. One was aggressive; the other—by nature—the warrior king of Tibet. That was unalterable. The words only give meaning to the fact.

The bites the older children had endured had been lessons—in the necessity for keeping distances and the art of creating nearnesses. A one-year-old, who crawls about the floors with abandonment, does not know the facts nor the words. Was it fair to wait for the truth? How many times could we avert the danger— the young boy, baby hands flailing affection; the dog with warning growl unheeded.

We did this right thing first.

If we advertised Lasha free to a good home, wouldn't the good home-keepers come running? We were honest in the advertisement: good watch dog; not good with small children. That sort of thing. Three people called. The first I wouldn't have given a hamster to and therefore I politely curtailed our discussion. The second one, despite our caution to take matters slowly, suddenly reached out a hand to pat Lasha on the head and withdrew the hand with a nearly truncated finger. It gave proof to the crookedness of the road we were on. The third, who was in her late sixties, decided seven-years-plus was really a tad too old; perhaps a puppy would be better.

There was really nothing very special about this dog. She was simply one of those dogs that grow up in a home, become part of the family's daily life, and then face a day like this.

Nothing special.

Except to Tamara . . . for theirs was truly a special affection. Perhaps it was the fact that they were the two youngest in the family, to this point, and had grown up together. It was Tammy's lap that Lasha sought out. Together they galloped along the street, blond hair snapping from each, racing each other under a summer sun. Perhaps because it was hardest for her, Tamara made her request.

Another month went by, and we did this second thing. And it couldn't be done right.

We had called the humane society. No, they couldn't place a dog that age, and especially not one that wasn't good with children, and definitely not one that nipped. We talked at length with our veterinarian. He explained the procedure. It would be gentle. No, there was no right way to do it. But pray, and cry, and worry about this small thing with the undershot jaw and the stubby legs who held a place in our lives. We had begged for the possibility of a way out, and none had been given.

So it was that we met in the family room, and talked it over, and wept in that small circle around a sleeping dog. And Tamara extracted that promise with her tears from her father's fearful heart: May I be the last to kiss Lasha goodbye?

I believe you were thinking of this that morning we drove to the veterinarian's office. Lasha had always been a house dog, the fierce defender of the hearth. She loathed anything on wheels, anything that didn't stay in place. The motion made her suddenly, irrevocably sick. This was a dog that needed four paws on steady ground. Unless you steadied her in the back seat of the car. It became a ritual, then. Whenever we had to travel to the vet's office for vaccinations or check-ups, you cradled Lasha in the back seat, stroked her ears, murmured comforting sounds to her. And kept a towel on your lap to soak up her nervous drooling. In such a way rituals become tradition, and thereby precious to us. And at this moment, also became a high calling which you so bravely fulfilled. You knew she would want those strokes of comfort, those last words. You also knew to what we were taking her. I believe you thought of that.

I thought of *these* things.

Strive as we might to keep suffering from us, we cannot. We travel the crooked road in this life. But it is a good thing: it is good we strive; it is also good we cannot keep suffering from us. We had known suffering before, acutely so. Then we longed for the commonplace, the dear accustomed routines, like darkness yearns for the dawning. A certain king who had suffered much knew this. He wrote: "Weeping may tarry for the night, but joy comes with the morning" (Psalm 30:5). Can one know the joy without the weeping? I think not. Not as something precious. How we despise suffering! How we loathe and hate it. And justly so. I remember years ago my father said to me—a passing remark that has never left me: "I don't trust a man who has never suffered." I didn't understand him then; I think that I, having suffered at different points on my own crooked road, having walked through the sea wondering with that same king whether God's way is in the sea, do understand that now. I understand that our suffering points us to a suffering so rude, so obscene it beggars the imagination. It is a stark cross thrown like a grotesque cry of pain against the sky over Golgotha. Then I see the man on that cross, with his arms open wide. I see him more clearly for having looked to him in suffering, begin to understand more clearly the reason for his suffering.

This I saw again that morning. And by this I began to understand again the narrowness of the way. My eyes squinted to the road, thinking of the vet's office ahead. I was also seeing you in the back seat, cradling Lasha in your arms, with the towel on your lap. I thought of another Mary who looked up to that scarecrow cross and wept. Tamara: Mary to the one who needs you now.

"Will it hurt Lasha at all, Daddy?"

"No, honey." I explained, once again, the procedure. Lasha knew the vet; she wouldn't be afraid. It wasn't as if we were turning her over to a stranger. He would inject her. She would fall asleep, then her heart would slow down and stop. "All she will feel is a little prick of the shot, and then she will fall asleep."

"Do you think she'll wake up in heaven?"

"Do you?"

"Yes."

"Then I think so too."

But do you understand the enormity of your question,

Tamara? You have thereby affirmed *your* being there.

A silence. Lasha panted, drooling, as she always did in the car. "Are you sure you want to come in, Tammy? If you like, I can go back in the office with Lasha and hold her while the doctor gives her the shot."

"No. I really want to kiss her goodbye."

And she did that hard thing, taking that unruly mop of hair in both hands and kissing her as she had so often done. She went the narrow way, the hard way—to its bitter end. And I witnessed the fiery torment of faith through fierce tears as blond head bent to blond head and the gift of love was bestowed on a love we could no longer hold fast to.

On the way home we stopped at a restaurant for a soft drink. "I don't want to go home until Lasha has died, Dad," Tamara said. We sat quietly there in the corner booth, watching cars on the street passing along a hurried way. I did tell her when Lasha had died. She bent her head and cried quietly.

Oh, my child. How I would protect you from suffering. But how grateful I am for that moment seared into my mind forever.

How the wind must have beat at the knob of that hill Golgotha and burned the cold tears on the cheeks of Mary. The rude scar of suffering, and our only hope of joy in the morning, etched there with arms nailed wide against the darkened sky.

From time to time, as we page through an old photo album and find there a picture of Lasha, freshly combed and shining, we think of that moment.

And a moment to come. In the morning.

Epilogue

It is now over two years since that June evening in 1985 when I admitted Pat to the hospital—a moment that dramatically changed the course of our lives.

It is a little over a year ago that I first approached Pat with the idea of writing this book. "Yes," she said, "but I don't want to read it." (She has since, and I'm grateful for her keen eye, particularly on technical points.) I wanted, at first, simply to refresh my memory on details by reading her journals. That, too, was a hard decision, to include them in this account. But real depression happens to real people. It isn't some mystical thing in the air. We agreed that large sections should go into this book, no matter how painful it was for us.

For me, it has been the hardest writing I have ever done. But it has been for Pat, too. Why did we do it?

It began with an urgent need. We recognized that many people whom we knew were afflicted or had been afflicted with this illness and didn't dare admit it openly. The illness is still shrouded in misunderstanding, and understanding is crucial to this illness, to surviving and to overcoming. We decided to write this, first of all, to provide understanding.

But there are also dozens of myths surrounding depression, a hodgepodge of false ideas that must be dispelled. They range from a frank misunderstanding of the illness itself to a distrust for different methods of treatment. The good news is that this illness can be treated, and others need to be aware of the methods of treatment.

Furthermore, for an illness that makes the sufferer feel abandoned by God, it is important to understand the spiritual dimensions of depression. Christians are often unwilling to admit to this feeling of abandonment, but it is a very real part of depression and has to be confronted and understood. When we affirm God's path in the sea, we confirm the richest mystery of God's grace. God also is the reality for real people.

Finally, we want people to know the good news that there is also a way out of the sea of depression. The time framework is different for each person. Hard facts must be confronted. The likelihood of a repeat occurrence increases dramatically for each individual occurrence of depression. For one who has suffered it, the fear is always there. But it can be overcome.

The normal duration for a major depressive episode such as Pat's is eighteen months. Her first attempt to go completely off medication, after about a year, was unsuccessful. She had been making genuine progress. Signs of improvement were clear and growing daily. Friends would comment often on how good it was to see the old sparkle in her eye, to hear her happy laughter, to see her involved in activities again. But behind the sparkle lay a shadow. For about a month, Pat struggled heroically without medication. She felt the claws of the beast raking inward. This time, at least; we were alert to its signals. Her psychiatrist decided to switch her to a different antidepressant. The renewed prescription seemed at first like a defeat.

"Will I ever get well?" Pat wondered aloud one evening. "Of course," I insisted. "But the main thing is that you feel well while you're getting well." I encouraged her with the progress she had made, then summoned my best voice of authority. "Look," I said, "it doesn't matter how long you have to be on medication. That isn't important. If it helps you, that's the main thing."

The new medication proved to be more effective than the first. Day by day the claws of the beast loosened, until the grip was broken. Pat no longer followed the daily routine of charting her feelings—they were leveling off into the normal patterns each of us feels. Her confidence grew. She made decisions about her own goals and aims. For example, for about five years she had been involved as a leader for an adult Bible study group at our church. She enjoyed that task, but her real longing—and gift—was to work with children. She became a Bible study leader for Story Hour—an evangelistic outreach for young children. God blessed the effort tremendously. It has continued into teaching Summer Vacation Bible School.

In this process she was making clear, direct decisions about *herself*, where her gifts lay and how best to use them. Moreover, the sparkle of that effervescent personality emerged with renewed and solid radiance. And the second medication went, almost unnoticed, from a peak, to a decrease, to a disappearance.

How we long for the commonplace! But we never really have that; life changes all about us with each minute of the day. Two years after that summer, Joel now romps in the wading pool at the park across the street, his mop of golden curls shining like a whirling sun. Life is an adventure, he reminds us, and he sallies forth in it from the dawn's breaking until too late at night. Then, while I read in one chair and Pat in another, Joel sits in his Pooh-Bag sleeper on the davenport, paging through an endless stack of books, most of them upside down, reciting wild stories he imagines belonging to the books. The energy is endless—for him—and he falls asleep at last from the sheer enervation of much living.

Having a two-year-old reminds us of the astonishing spiritual perception of very young children. I had forgotten those years and that action with our older children. Once, three-year-old Jeff forgot to pray before I gave him his lunch, and I reminded him. Faultlessly he prayed the Lord's prayer, the first time he had ever done so. It staggered me with the crushing responsibility of training children in the way they should go. As parents, we stand in the place of God himself to our children.

With Joel, the fact was reinforced in a new way. It so happened that Jeff and I made separate trips to New York a week apart, I as a speaker at a Christian college, Jeff on a tour with his high school drama troupe. A ritual started. Whenever an airplane winged overhead Joel asked, "Going to New York?" And then, for assurance, he would ask, "A man driving that airplane?" Yes, we assured him, someone was driving the airplane. Someone was in charge. Someone had care over that airplane.

It happened at this time that Joel developed a fear of thunderstorms. When one burst during the daytime we watched the rain, commenting that Jesus had sent it to grow the flowers. After one spectacular roll of thunder, Joel asked, "Who's driving the thunder?"

Pat responded, "Jesus drives the thunder, Joel." Thereafter, whenever it stormed, Joel commented, "Jesus drives the thunder."

Yes, even in the thunder, someone is in control. The grace of having older children is that Pat and I can get away together, at least one evening each week, and have built-in babysitters. Betsy and Tammy, whose lives are showered with diversions, are never unwilling to pause in their hectic paces and babysit for us. They gladly turn down other jobs to do so.

And there are surprises. Who would expect a brother approaching sixteen to be best of friends with his baby brother? Each afternoon Jeff and Joel share a ritual. When Jeff gets home from school, before doing his paper route, he finds a can of soda for himself and a bottle for Joel, gathers his little brother in his huge arms, and takes him down to the family room where they sprawl in the old leather chair to watch a half hour of cartoons on TV. From my study I hear them, one a young man who now almost outweighs me, and the other a young boy who can almost outrun me, laughing hilariously over their cartoons.

Only one physical change marks our lives—an odd one, but with a certain final lesson for us.

We have vowed our lives to servanthood, and against opulence. True, on a teacher's salary this is not a difficult task. We also remember that time, many years ago, when the caseworker for our adoption of Jeff inquired about our financial situation. Grace prevailed then; it has not forsaken us since. To live a life of servanthood, we believe, also includes financial sacrifice. So it was that we believed we could get along on one car, even when the six of us shoehorned into our eight-year-old Oldsmobile like six toes in a too-tight shoe. We began to doubt the wisdom of our vow. With four children now, Pat needed the car to hustle them to piano lessons, medical appointments, and a score of other obligations. So I took the bus to work—except for those days when it was pouring rain, or a Michigan blizzard spumed, or I had committee meetings late into the evening. So it was that we came upon the beater.

What is a beater?

In the beginning it was a car. Someone bought it; polished, gassed, tuned it. Laid out good money for it in 1976.

It came to me free of charge, a gift from a benevolent brother-in-law. There were expenses, of course. Replacing the front brake was necessary since the caliper was locked and the wheel wouldn't turn. But, never one to look a gift beater under the hood, I took it.

My first indication that I had something more than just an old car came when I drove it home. Jeff came out to examine this noise, this clank and rattle, this incredible hulk of metal inching up the driveway, locked wheel sending smoke signals to Sioux Falls.

"That's sweeeet!" he murmured in rapturous tones.

"Well," I said, "maybe we could get some filler and patch up the rust holes. Make that a few buckets of filler."

"Dad," he reproved me, "the rust makes the car. Don't touch it!" Not one to dispute the wisdom of one soon to be awarded his first driver's license, I learned my first lesson in the qualities of a quality beater. It must have sufficient rust. But in the right places. The top, for example, must be rusted. Rocker panels are par; holes in the quarter panels acceptable; a straight sight-line from the trunk to the street beneficial; but a *quality* beater must have rust on the roof.

Where had I gone wrong? When I was his age I polished the red hood of my father's Ford until it glowed like the afterburner of an F-111.

"When I get my license," Jeff said, "this is the car I drive." It was a command. Betsy and Tammy immediately vowed they would never be seen in this thing. When forced to, of necessity, they rode with their heads ducked.

I had the brake fixed. And, although it ran respectably, I decided to change the plugs and replace the valve gasket that spewed a vicious stream of oil over the spark plugs. The gasket was no problem. I did it in four hours—a task, I have since learned, that takes a mechanic about fifteen minutes. The plugs were indeed a problem. Tucked away at impossible angles, they were neither moved by my diction or gestures. I waved the socket wrench to no discernible effect. It actually had to contact a plug to turn it, but contact, like some Freshman English classes I have known, was impossible. They were glacially unmoved by my most exquisite imprecations.

I must confess to some down moments regarding this beater. But the longer I have it and have studied it, like the hard, unyielding surface of a term paper, I have begun to penetrate its aura, its mystique, its incomparable "sweetness." And have made certain deductions. A classic beater, I now understand, is characterized by certain immutable laws, the first of which is aesthetically pleasing rust which I have mentioned and which I shall not, under Jeffrey's law, touch. These others come to mind.

A beater should not be washed. Ever. Mud should streak the lower portion, rain-film the upper. But, it is a good thing to clean the worn whitewalls, the better to accentuate the uneven tread. The chrome ornament on the hood, which must be broken, should be free of rust if at all possible.

A beater should have several, five or six, wires hanging from under the dashboard. Preferably they should not be connected to anything observable. One or more should have a strange orange capsule on the end. Under no circumstances should these be tucked back under the dashboard. Their function is to hang there.

The doors on a beater do not lock. This is so that if anyone steals the radio, which doesn't work, they will not break any glass.

A beater has (required) over 100,000 miles. There is no special glory in having over 200,000. That is irrelevant.

But it must have turned over at least once and register a nice figure like 9,000 miles on the odometer.

A beater must have the original paint job, but it must be sun- and salt-bleached several different hues. Crazed enamel is perfectly acceptable. Thinned paint is excellent. Never, ever, should a beater be repainted, unless it is repainted silver. I have seen several excellent silver beaters.

But above all, it must have that certain aesthetic magic, the thing that makes an instructor give an A on a term paper, the thing that makes a boy with palms itchy for the keys exclaim, "It's sweeeet!"

Then you can park it in front of the house, on the street, bravely. Glance out upon it fondly at bedtime. See the streetlamp refract in the rust. And whisper how sweet it is.

One would not be hardpressed to make an analogy: life is quite often like this beater. Our tread wears unevenly, and sometimes the engine becomes ornery. Life has a price; it is seldom a gilded road of ease.

But the analogy doesn't hold. While my beater—Jeff's beater—will one day, probably soon, be hauled off to the junk yard, life is precious. Each one of us will confront some sea of conflict. It may be the disquiet waters by the sea's edge or the roar and rip of the deep sea's undertow. But that isn't the end of the story. It never is. That great grace of God which aligned the foundations of this world still plumbs the seas of our lives, denying the power of darkness. He has made the sea; his path will be in it.

It will deny the sting of death also. For when this earthly sojourn is through, the Christian conviction asserts that there is not the troubled sea but the Sea of Crystal, flowing from the throne of God. That is the great story, the final chapter in each of our Christian lives, the one that makes all the pages here on earth simply a preface for the greatest story ever to be told. Finally, his path is *that* Sea, shining and glorious in the light of the Bright Morning Star.

Appendix
Questions and Answers about Depression and Related Illnesses

W hile we have tried to answer many of the questions about depression in the text of this book, many questions remain. Depression is an illness of many faces and variations. This concluding chapter raises some of the more common questions about depression and related illnesses. It does not intend to be thorough or a replacement for professional counseling. The index below serves as a guide to subject areas.

Question:

1. *Why are so many specialized medical terms used with depression?*

Basically because there are so many varieties of depression, and it is a highly individual illness. Generally, depression falls under the broad medical category called *affective disorders*, which simply means "mood disorders." The DSM III, *Diagnostic and Statistical Manual of Mental Disorders*, Third Edition (Washington, D.C.: American Psychiatric Association, 1980), defines these as follows: "The essential feature of this group of disorders is a disturbance of mood, accompanied by a full or partial manic or depressive syndrome, that is not due to any other physical or mental disorder. Mood refers to a prolonged emotion that colors the whole psychic life; it generally involves either depression or elation."

2. *What is the difference between "manic episode" and "major depressive episode?"*

The distinction here is also called bipolar (manic) and unipolar (major depressive). Essentially, in the manic episode the person's mood swings between elevated (or manic) stages and depressed stages. DSM III supplies the following as partial indications for diagnostic criteria for a manic episode:

A. One or more distinct periods with a predominantly elevated, expansive, or irritable mood. The elevated or irritable mood must be a prominent part of the illness and relatively persistent although it may alternate or intermingle with depressive mood.

B. Duration of at least one week (or any duration if hospitalization is necessary), during which, for most of the time, at least three of the following symptoms have persisted (four if the mood is only irritable) and have been present to a significant degree:

1) increase in activity (either socially, at work, or sexually) or physical restlessness
2) more talkative than usual or pressure to keep talking
3) flight of ideas or subjective experience that thoughts are racing
4) inflated   self-esteem   (grandiosity, which may be delusional)
5) decreased need for sleep.
6) distractibility, i.e., attention is too easily drawn to unimportant or irrelevant external stimuli
7) excessive involvement in activities that have a high potential for painful consequences which is not recognized, e.g., buying sprees, sexual indiscretions, foolish business investments, reckless driving. The "major depressive episode" or unipolar depression is marked by a progressive, severe experience of depression.

3. *Do artists seem particularly afflicted by manic disorders?*

Ever since the ancient Greeks, people have speculated on the link between creativity and manic depression. Shakespeare writes that "melancholy is the nurse of frenzy," an early description of manic depression. Coleridge called it "grief without a pang." Writers such as Emily Dickinson and Samuel Johnson are thought to have been manic depressive. Manic depressive composers include Handel, Schumann, Berlioz, and Mahler. Twentieth-century American poets include Robert Lowell, Delmore Schwartz, Randall Jarrell, Theodore Roethke, John Berryman, Sylvia Plath, and Anne Sexton. Frederick Goodwin, scientific director of the National Institute of Mental Health, says that 38 percent of Pulitzer Prize-winning poets meet the DSM III criteria for manic depressive.

4. *Have any clinical studies been performed?*

Psychology Today reported on one of the more recent studies in its April, 1987 issue. Nancy C. Andreasen, a psychiatrist with the University of Iowa College of Medicine, "completed a study of fifteen topflight American writers at the prestigious University of Iowa Writers' Workshop and compared them with others matched for age, education, and sex. Ten of the writers had histories of mood disorders, compared with only two from the comparison group. Two of the ten were diagnosed as manic depressive, and almost all reported mood swings, including manic or hypomanic (mildly manic) states." Andreasen has continued her study for fifteen years, reinforcing her findings that creative artists do suffer a higher incidence of mood disorders.

5. *What causes this?*

Some of the more common answers include these:

1) In temperament, artists frequently tend to be more sensitive to a wide range of stimuli.
2) The creative activity of artists can achieve a pattern of intense effort followed by exhaustion, a pattern similar to manic depression.
3) Some researchers speculate that artists have less psychological inhibition in exploring the unconscious, thereby permitting greater freedom of the unconscious to direct mental activities.
4) Artists typically have greater powers of concentration, and the ability to focus intensely on imaginative experiences. This may correlate with the manic state of manic depression which is characterized by free-flowing associations.

6. *What are the criteria for unipolar depression or "a major depressive episode"?*

These criteria are also discussed in chapters 2 and 3, but the DSM III provides a short list as a diagnostic guideline. It defines the major depressive episode as follows:

A. Dysphoric mood or loss of interest or pleasure in all or almost all usual activities and pastimes. The dysphoric mood is characterized by symptoms such as the following: feeling depressed, sad, blue, hopeless, low, down in the dumps, irritable. . . .

B. At least four of the following symptoms have each been present nearly every day for a period of at least two weeks [criteria selected as applying to adults].

1) poor appetite or significant weight loss (when not dieting) or increased appetite or significant weight gain
2) insomnia or hypersomnia
3) psychomotor agitation or retardation
4) loss of interest or pleasure in usual activities, or decrease in sexual drive
5) loss of energy; fatigue
6) feelings of worthlessness, self-reproach, or excessive or inappropriate guilt
(7) complaints or evidence of diminished ability to think or concentrate, such as slowed thinking, or indecisiveness
(8) recurrent thoughts of death, suicidal ideation, wishes to be dead, or suicide attempt.

In clinical analysis of depression there are, of course, symptoms that extend beyond these and also subdivisions of these. For example, in *Depression: Causes and Treatment* (Philadelphia: University of Pennsylvania Press, 1967), Dr. Aaron T. Beck distinguishes what he calls "The Primary Triad in Depression." These would relate to cognitive signs, or ways in which we view ourselves and the world. Dr. Beck sets forth his triad as follows:

> The first component of the triad is the pattern of construing experiences in a negative way. The patient consistently interprets his interactions with his environment as representing defeat, deprivation, or disparagement. He sees his life as filled with a succession of burdens, obstacles, or traumatic situations, all of which detract from him in a significant way.

The second component is the pattern of viewing himself in a negative way. He regards himself as deficient, inadequate, or unworthy, and tends to attribute his unpleasant experiences to a physical, mental, or moral defect in himself. Furthermore, he regards himself as undesirable and worthless because of his presumed defect, and tends to reject himself because of it.

The third component consists of viewing the future in a negative way. He anticipates that his current difficulties of suffering will continue indefinitely. As he looks ahead, he sees a life of unremitting hardship, frustration, and deprivation. (p. 225)

Thus, this negative pattern, according to Beck, affects an individual's perception of life, of himself, and of his future.

7. *How important a factor is heredity in depression?*

A person will not "inherit" depression, but research indicates a genetic predisposition to it. People with a history of depression in the family should be alert to signs of it in themselves. Referring to a recent study by Myrna Weissman, director of the depression research unit at Yale School of Medicine, Winifred Gallagher, in her essay "The Dark Affliction of the Mind and Body," *Discover* (May, 1986), speculates on this connection. Gallagher writes: "The high incidence of depression among those most likely to be parents suggests ominous consequences for future generations. Weissman's studies indicate that children with one depressed parent are two to three times as likely to suffer from depression by age 18 as children of well parents; if both parents are depressed, their children are four to six times as likely to develop the disease." (p. 67) Gallagher may paint a bleaker picture than is warranted; nonetheless, people do well to be aware of a history of depression in their families.

8. *What is a "Major Depression, Recurrent?"*

Approximately 50 percent of persons with a major depression will eventually suffer another episode. If another episode appears, it is described as recurrent.

9. *What is "masked" depression?*

The patient "masks" or hides the depression by complaining of physiological ailments as causes for discomfort or the bad moods. The patient may wear the "mask" of smiling; therefore it is also called "smiling depression." The denial of emotions generally leads to an intense sense of loss and lifelessness.

10. *I am confused about other terms. For example, I hear about "biological depression" and "chemical imbalance."*

The distinction between them is between cause and condition, between what the textbooks call "etiology" (or origins) and the resulting illness. A biological depression occurs when the primary source for the depression is biological dysfunction. Other possible causes, such as drug abuse, stress, or bad relationships are not primary causes. A chemical imbalance, the dysfunction of hormonal processes in the brain, is one physiological manifestation of the illness.

11. *Can drug abuse cause depression?*

Drug abuse can contribute to mood disorders. One of the most notorious drugs used is cocaine. One doctor commented that using the smallest amount of cocaine is the psychological equivalent of playing Russian roulette without knowing how many bullets are in the chamber. One experience can lead to suicidal depression.

12. *How many people suffer from depression?*

Since so many people manage to hide their depression, and since so many people suffer varying degrees of depression short of requiring medical treatment, precise figures are impossible.

Generally accepted figures are that 1 out of 4 individuals suffers some form of mood disorder in a lifetime. In the adult population approximately 12 percent of men and 18 percent of females have had a major depressive episode at some time. Approximately 3 percent of men and 6 percent of females have had an episode serious enough to require hospitalization.

Depression is the major diagnosis for approximately 25 percent of patients in public mental institutions, 40 percent in outpatient psychiatric clinics, 50 percent in private psychiatric facilities. Depression represents 70 percent of the psychiatric diagnosis in nonpsychiatric medical practice.

Figures for adolescents are uncertain.

13. *How is depression treated?*

Generally depression is treated by a two-fold program of therapy (counseling) and medication. Depending upon the nature of the depression, medication may or may not be necessary.

Most bipolar, or manic depressive, patients are treated with lithium carbonate, a metallic element that affects the chemistry of the brain. Common brand names for lithium include Eskalith, Lithone, Lithonate, Lithotabs, Pfi-Lithium. This drug has been found to be both remedial, that is, it helps correct the chemical dysfunction, and preventative, working to prevent future recurrences of the manic-depressive syndrome. As with many antidepressants, the drug may be prescribed for a long period of time, not unusually for several years. The success of the drug, however, has been remarkable, when the patient cooperates with the doctor's prescribed treatment.

For patients suffering from unipolar depression, the

doctor may select from two common antidepressants. Less frequently used are the MAO-I (Monoamine Oxidase Inhibitors), which have more side effects and require stricter dietary guidelines than the more commonly prescribed Tricyclic antidepressants. Tricyclics, of which there are many generic and brand names, help control and correct the chemical action of norepinephrine or serotonin in the neuron, helping restore the normal chemical balance.

Like all drugs, antidepressants have side effects, most frequently a drying of different membranes. The patient may have a dry mouth, dry, itchy eyes, and may have to take a stool softener such as Ducosate Sodium to relieve constipation. Most antidepressants have a mild sedative effect, which is helpful to restore regular sleep patterns disrupted by the illness. Some patients may experience a degree of trembling or weakness, some confusion, and an effect on heart rate and blood pressure. Often the patient will not be permitted to exercise hard because of the effect on blood pressure.

Hospitalization may be necessary in more severe cases when the person is unable to function in his or her normal routines or when suicidal tendencies become evident.

14. *What if I'm depressed, but avoid treatment because I'm afraid of being hospitalized?*

The vast majority of depressed persons are successfully treated on an outpatient basis; that is, by regular counseling, and medication when it is necessary. Don't let a fear of hospitalization prevent you from seeking help.

15. *Is it necessary to have Christian counseling for depression?*

In *Toward a Christian Psychotherapy* (Cherry Hill, N.J.: Mack Publishing Co., 1973), Theodore Jansma asks, "Where shall the troubled Christian go for help?" In response to his question, Jansma builds a case for the Christian patient to seek help from a Christian psychotherapist. He points out that "we must keep clearly in mind that a Christian psychotherapy is only an intermediate objective. It is a method for achieving another objective; it is in the service of Christian whole-ness." He adds that "the troubled Christian must be helped to become an untroubled *Christian*." (p. 60)

This is sound advice. If one has a choice, it is preferable that a Christian patient seek a Christian psychotherapist, given similar professional expertise with that of a non-Christian psychotherapist. The questions about belief, guilt, security, and health have to be dealt with in the context of biblical truth. While a humanistic psychiatrist might dismiss all guilt as meaningless, the Christian needs to distinguish between guilt incurred as part of the illness and legitimate guilty feelings over sin. While the humanist psychiatrist might encourage one to feel good about oneself, the Christian needs to know that he or she is forgiven and that Jesus loves him, that he is precious in the eyes of the one who has said, "I will never fail you nor forsake you" (Hebrews 13:5). At the same time, one must acknowledge that, failing the avail-ability of a Christian psychotherapist, the person who is ill must seek out the best help possible, relying in this case upon God to work through those means.

16. *I have a very close friend who has all the signs of depression. His wife keeps making excuses: "Jim is getting over the flu." "Jim is just tired." Yet, this has gone on for over six weeks. Is there anything I can do?*

We are legitimately fearful of two things here. First, we don't want to play amateur psychiatrist and diagnose an illness for someone else. Second, we are hesitant to interfere in the private lives of friends or relatives. Yet, we observe an ongoing problem and want to help. How do we proceed?

First, try to find out the exact nature of Jim's condition. It is important to be sure of Jim's need. As we stated in the caution above, far too many people start playing amateur psychiatrist with other people's problems. A little knowledge can be a very dangerous thing. If you see Jim often enough, and know him well enough, and if he does exhibit signs of depression as discussed here, then it would seem that you have cause to be concerned.

Secondly, try to find out if anything is being done. Find a way to contact the spouse and, very discreetly, express your concern for Jim's health. Without necessarily asking about the illness you can ascertain whether Jim is under medical care. For example, you can say, "Jim has really been down a long time. Have you taken him to a doctor? Is he still seeing a doctor?" In such a way you can determine whether Jim is receiving medical care. Understand that the spouse's "excuses" about his condition are very likely due to our cultural fear of admitting to depression. It may very well be that Jim is receiving proper care, but the family doesn't know how to relate this. If this is the case, you can simply offer your assistance as needed and assure the spouse of your continued prayers on Jim's behalf.

Should the case be that your friend or relative is receiving insufficient medical attention, or no professional care, you may sense the need to do more. The third step would be to try to find some intermediary. Does Jim have a pastor or a very close friend who is knowledgeable about depression and who could counsel the couple about receiving appropriate care? If Jim has seen a family doctor once, but has not followed up, it is not unusual for someone to consult the doctor with a concern about the patient.

If a suitable intermediary cannot be located, it may become your responsibility to discuss with—or even to confront—the couple about the situation. This should be nonthreatening and in a spirit of loving concern. You may wish to have an informed pastor accompany you. Come prepared with some knowledge of symptoms and medical resources for treatment both as discussed in this book and as available in your community. Nothing is worse than to identify a problem, then to sit there wondering what to do about it. If you must do this, do it with this conviction: Any risk is preferable to the risks of a depression untreated.

17. *My depression came about through bad relationships. I still can't forgive the person who caused me this pain.*

Once we put aside all the easy clichés about forgiveness, we recognize the hard reality of the act of forgiveness. Why? Because the wrong done to us still causes pain. It is hard to forgive someone even while that person continues to hurt you, or if that person doesn't seem to realize or care that he has hurt you in the past. And that hurt may linger weeks, even years, after the action.

Sometimes the situation is further complicated by the fact that the lingering hurt has been done by someone we are very close to, someone whom we love very much and want to love wholly—without the screen of this hurt. Sometimes the hasty word, the impulsive act, the sudden sin of a parent, a child, a loved one can cut a scar into that relationship that seems to go all the deeper because it is a violation of love and trust.

Recognizing the hard act of forgiveness, we also recognize the necessity for it. There can be no genuine psychological or spiritual health apart from forgiveness both of ourselves and by ourselves for others. In *Forgive and Forget* (New York: Harper & Row, 1984), Lewis B. Smedes describes forgiveness as surgery: "When you forgive someone for hurting you, you perform spiritual surgery inside your soul; you cut away the wrong that was done to you so that you can see your 'enemy' through the magic eyes that can heal your soul."

In addition to reading this remarkable book, the person who struggles with hurt and forgiveness may need the leading of others toward forgiveness. It is wise to seek pastoral or professional counseling for these hurts.

18. *Why did God allow my depression to happen?*

Although no one can know the mind of God, some answers to this crucial question for the depressed Christian are offered in Chapter 9.

We must distinguish, however, between *cause* and *permission*. Depression is not caused by God. Rather, depression is caused by our inevitable and inescapable participation in a fallen world. Every sin has bad effects—both upon the sinner and upon the innocent. Also, because of our fallen condition we experience those bad effects psychologically, physiologically, and spiritually.

19. *But couldn't God have prevented it?*

Indeed he could have. But he chose not to. Just as God permitted evil to occur to Job (and it was not caused by God but by Satan), so too God permitted this to happen to you. This understanding brings us to the crucible of faith and trust. At such times when rational understanding fails us, we rely upon the conviction of faith. We believe, as James tells us, that "the testing of your faith produces steadfastness" (James 1:3). We believe that God will have a good end for our bad times.

At any time of testing it is indeed difficult to see that "good end." At such times, however, we are given scriptural patterns and promises that ground our belief and give it substance. Job was led through his trial to a good end. David was led through the desert to a place of God's rest. Jesus was led through Gethsemane and Golgotha to the Resurrection.

We wish that we did not have to endure suffering. But the biblical models, particularly as discussed in

Hebrews 11, assure us of the necessity for faith during our affliction.

The models are affirmed, furthermore, by God's promises, which the Christian can cling to with assurance. God will be with you in your suffering (Isaiah 41:10-13 and 43:1-3). God will never forsake you or leave you. He will strengthen your drooping hands and weak knees (Hebrews 12:12). God does care about you (1 Peter 5:7). God does love you (1 John 4:13-18). And God will remove the suffering from you (Revelation 21:4).

20. *Who am I? In my depression I feel as though I have lost my self. Will I ever be the same person with the same personality I formerly had?*

The loss of self-worth and a sense of identity is surely one of the most excruciating experiences of depression. The fears induced by that loss are very real ones and your question drives to the heart of those fears.

Perhaps the question can best be answered by means of an analogy. While analogies don't provide logical proof, they do help us understand the significance and meaning of an experience.

Depression is an illness that changes the way we are, but not the person we are. Consider that basic fact in terms of this analogy. If someone broke an arm, for some time the full use of that arm would be lost. If it is a severe break, the person may very well wonder if the arm will ever be the same.

Two things bear upon the analogy. First, the broken arm is still an arm—not a leg, or a rib, or a hipbone. It will not cease being an arm by having been broken. So too the person ill with depression, although feeling useless and having lost a sense of personhood during the illness, does not cease being the *person* he or she is because of the illness.

Second, the arm will mend. Indeed, by careful therapy, the arm may even be stronger than it was before.

Yet, although the person may in future years even forget
that the arm was broken, the person can never deny
that at one time the arm was broken. The arm may function normally, and respond readily and efficiently to the
commands the brain sends to it. Yet that arm was once
undeniably broken and, however thoroughly healthy
and healed, something in the bone will be different for
having been broken.

So too, the depressed person can, and very likely will,
regain full health. The personality will emerge intact,
healthy and healed, as the arm did. Yet we also recognize
that the *experience* of the illness of depression is undeniable. It would be unrealistic to suggest otherwise. The
experience of depression will have been absorbed into
the personality and be a part of if. Even though the
illness is healed, the experience will have its effect. Often,
this can make the personality, like the arm, stronger for
having undergone the illness. In short, then, although
the experience and memory of depression will be a part
of your personhood, your essential personality will recover from the illness. You will be who you have always
been, but as with all events during life's journey, you
will have grown and will have been changed by the
experience.

21. *What is an anxiety or "panic" attack?*

The anxiety or panic attack is now recognized as an
illness separate from depression but very much like it.
While depression may very well bear periods of acute
anxiety, the illness itself is the primary phenomenon,
and the anxiety is one of its symptoms or manifestations.
Yet, people who are not clinically depressed may also
bear brief periods of excruciating anxiety.

In *Depression: Causes and Treatment*, Dr. Aaron Beck
distinguishes anxiety as a disorder allied with depression
but differing according to cognitive content, or how a

person perceives life and self. According to Beck, the primary cognitive sign of a depressive disorder is a "negative concept of self, world, and future." The primary cognitive sign of anxiety attack is the acute "concept of personal danger." (p. 270)

Anxiety may be understood as persistent and undue nervousness, such as worrying that a pain in your side is a tumor. Persistent anxiety interprets customary stimuli or experiences in the worst possible way. If an anxious person hears a siren, he is convinced his house is burning down.

This "concept of personal danger" begins to sound very much like a phobia, but with a significant difference. People suffering from phobias experience the sense of danger in specific *and* avoidable situations.

Anxiety attacks are different from phobias or customary, ongoing anxiety. In the anxiety attack the person suddenly and overwhelmingly feels helpless, threatened, and vulnerable. The person feels stripped of defense mechanisms. A sudden surge of fear rips through them. Uncontrollable crying may overtake them. The person's pulse often accelerates, sometimes wildly. The person under anxiety attack may curl into a fetal position in retreat from the imagined danger.

22. *What leads to anxiety attacks?*

In *The Anxiety Disease* (New York: Scribners, 1983), David V. Sheehan, M.D., identifies two types of anxiety. Like some forms of depression, anxiety may be stimulated by external (exogenous) events. Sheehan describes this type: "The first is the type normally experienced as a reaction to the stress of danger, when a person can clearly identify a threat to his (or her) security or safety . . ." (p. 9) Also like some forms of depression, the second type is produced from within (endogenous), and it is this type that we call the anxiety attack. Sheehan describes this phenomenon: "Evidence now accumulating suggests that this second anxiety condition is a disease, whose victims appear to be born with a genetic vulnerability to it. It usually starts with spasms of anxiety that strike suddenly, without warning, and for no apparent reason." (p. 9) The person suffering the attack, in addition to the reactions described above, may suffer from dizziness, shortness of breath, and trembling.

23. *How common are anxiety attacks?*

Sheehan asserts that anxiety attacks of the second type afflict as much as 5 percent of the general population, and that for as much as 1 percent of the general population it is a disabling illness. Approximately 80 percent of its victims are female, with the highest frequency rate between the ages of twenty to thirty. It is caused, he writes, by an interplay of three forces: biological, psychological conditioning, and stress.

24. *How are anxiety attacks treated?*

As this condition has received greater attention as an illness allied with depression but separable from it, it has called for its own course of medical and pharmaceutical treatment. Frequently, a combination of an antidepressant such as amiltryptyline and a tranquilizer will be used. One of the most rapidly effective drugs now used, according to Dr. Sheehan, is alprazdam, recognized as one of the least disruptive and least toxic alternatives.

As with depression, it should be recognized that when anxiety attacks afflict one member of the family, the entire family is involved: "The life of an entire family is severely affected when one member has the anxiety disease, and the support of that family can play a role in long-term recovery." (p. 177) One of the greatest dangers for the family is the sense of guilt that they are somehow to blame for the attacks. But, Dr. Sheehan adds, "it is especially hard on the victims. They are blamed for a weakness and they feel weak. Yet they know they cannot will the disease away. They feel guilty for what they cannot do. They become depressed about the life they are missing, aware that it is slipping away from them. They feel hopeless, helpless, and worthless." (p. 179)

The person suffering from anxiety attacks requires an acute degree of sensitivity, but also clear, objective leading. The same care that the Christian community extends toward the depressed should be extended toward the person suffering from anxiety attacks in terms of understanding, support, and encouragement. Especially, the person must be made aware of his or her intrinsic worthiness as a child of God.

25. *Suicide among teenagers is much in the news. Is suicide more common, or do we just hear more about it?*

Suicide is indeed a most serious and growing phenomenon among teenagers. According to Dr. Seymour Perkins, chairman of the National Youth Suicide Center in Washington, D.C., as many as two million people between the ages of 13-19 will *attempt* suicide each year.

Nearly 6,000 deaths by suicide are reported in the United States each year, but the actual figure is estimated to be much higher, possibly as many as 20,000.

Suicide hasn't been a problem unique to teenagers. Until recently, men over sixty-five held the highest rate for an age group. That distinction now has passed to people in their twenties, but the suicide rate among teenagers has soared dramatically.

The National Center for Health Statistics estimates that in 1984, the latest year for which complete statistics are available, 9 of every 100,000 teenagers between 15-19 killed themselves, a total of 1,692. That same year, 15.6 of every 100,000 Americans aged 20-24, 3,334 people, committed suicide. For both groups the rates are increasing. From 1950 to 1977, the suicide rate for males aged 15-19 quadrupled; for females in the same age category the rate doubled. During the last decade, the rate for all teenagers tripled.

Males are three times more likely to kill themselves than females, although more females will attempt suicide.

26. *What is the relationship between suicide and depression?*

For some depressed people, the loss of self-worth is so acute that they genuinely believe the world would be a better place without them. In severe depression, persons sometimes hear voices telling them they are worthless, that they would be better off dead, that they should kill themselves. Some depressed persons even plot in careful detail the ways in which they would commit suicide.

While suicide is a legitimate fear for the severely depressed person, not all depressed persons who have these feelings will commit suicide, nor will all people who commit suicide suffer from severe depression. As with most mental illnesses, the risk of suicide is higher with a family history of suicide or deep depression.

Since suicide victims share many of the same warning signs as depressed persons, families should be alert to the signs in either case.

27. *What signals a potential suicide?*

For every person who commits suicide, anywhere from 10 to 100 others attempt suicide. Moreover, experts say that as many as 80 percent of those attempting suicide warn people beforehand, sometimes very openly. One-third to one-half of suicides have made prior attempts.

Several of the major symptoms of depression apply also to suicide: sudden changes in appetite and sleep patterns, moodiness, withdrawal, fatigue, loss of interest in hobbies or previously pleasurable events, impulsive behavior.

Suicide is often triggered by a stressful or humiliating event which breaks an already fragile self-esteem. Drug and alcohol abuse have recently been seen to play contributory roles. Children of divorce are at risk. About 71 percent of young people who attempt suicide are from broken homes.

Potential suicides may give away prized possessions, and let slip remarks such as, "You'd be better off if I were dead"; "I'm worthless"; "Life isn't worth it"; "You'll be sorry—or miss me—when I'm gone."

While certain of these signs are not an unusual part of teenage behavior, if a person demonstrates a combination of these signs over a period of two or more weeks, need for professional intervention is urgent.

28. What are "copycat" suicides?

This is largely a phenomenon among young people, 15-20 years old. News of a suicide often triggers others to follow the pattern, thus the "copycat" syndrome. The syndrome raises several other questions.

One wonders if it is good or bad for the media to give coverage of suicides. Some people claim that the news simply triggers more suicides. But it is also true that news coverage draws attention to problems, and that many young people have received help because of the increased media coverage.

The phenomenon of "copycat" suicide raises other questions. Why would someone follow the pattern? People contemplating suicide have typically lost a sense of self-worth and long for attention. When, through their deaths, some people have attracted tremendous media attention, the potential suicide might now see this as the opportunity to insist upon or to mandate attention.

Suicides often have three compelling motivations: 1) to escape some personal hurt or pain; 2) to hurt someone else by their deaths; 3) to attract attention by their deaths. The sad fact is that the suicide doesn't know if he or she has achieved these ends or not.

29. *A potential suicide might be reading these very words. What one piece of advice would you give that person?*

At this point in your life reasoning doesn't make much sense to you. You can't seem to find reasons to go on living. I understand that.

I also understand that at this moment your world looks absolutely hopeless, and because of that you are desperate. Death seems a way out. Perhaps you are afraid of the hurt that death will cause you but it seems preferable to the hurt you are living with each day.

But understand this: Death is final. If you are desperate, you can also exercise the alternative of calling for help. No matter how hopeless the world seems, there are people who will help you.

Understand also that there has never, ever been a person who, upon receiving help, has not been glad that he or she is still alive.

If everything seems hopeless, what do you have to lose by asking for help?

If you have a telephone book nearby, look in the advertising section under CRISIS INTERVENTION SERVICE or under SUICIDE. Trained counselors at such help agencies can provide help. Secondly, you can call a pastor at any church, a counseling service (also listed under the advertising section of the phone book), or a local police department. The police are trained for crisis intervention.

30. *Can suicides be spiritually saved? That is, can they go to heaven? Or is suicide an unpardonable sin?*

The question is difficult to answer, because the final answer lies in the mind of God, and no human can pretend to know that mind fully.

The question is difficult to answer, furthermore, because the Bible gives so little guidance on it. It is one of those issues where we trust God's wisdom and love. If one researches Scripture for an answer, one receives little firm direction. One might say that the person who has killed himself has violated the express commandment of God, but surely this is a different kind of killing than, say, the premeditated murder of another person. Scripture records several suicides. Of these, Samson was one of God's chosen leaders.

Having researched, worked with, and experienced the illness of depression during several years now, we find another way to respond to the question. The suicide is, in many cases, afflicted by acutely depressive moods. The loss of self-worth may be so acute that the "person" has virtually ceased to exist. The person who kills himself is often the victim of an illness over which he has little or no control, and therefore cannot be held responsible for his action.

In an article in *Christianity Today*, (March 20, 1987), Thomas D. Kennedy, Professor of religion at Hope College, writes on this question:

> If we define suicide as consisting of only free and uncoerced actions, we must ask a series of questions as we try to understand any particular suicide: To what extent do we know that a suicide in question was genuinely free? Could pain (either physical or emotional) have coerced the individual to do what he otherwise would not have done? But even if we could know that an act of suicide was genuinely free, can we know that the aim of the act was indeed one's own death rather than a misguided cry for help? Can we know that the suicide believed this action would really kill? (p. 22)

Kennedy points out that rational understanding and theology cannot comprehend the complexities of suicidal depression, that the suicide sees life differently than a rational, healthy person. The suicide may even see the act as a means of coming close to God: "In many cases suicide is mistakenly chosen to bring one nearer to God. We cannot say that such a motive for suicide is correct. Nor can we say that a person who makes this tragic mistake has removed herself forever from the grace of God." (p. 23)

31. *Are the elderly more susceptible to depression?*

According to the comprehensive study *Depression and Aging*, (New York: Springer Publishers, 1983), "the incidence of depression is particularly significant in persons 65 and older not only for depressive disorders but also for transient symptoms of depression." (p. 17)

32. *Why? What contributes to this higher incidence?*

In addition to the greater likelihood of general health problems, the elderly are under particular pressure from stress factors related to depression. Such factors include the following:

—Decreased social interaction. The elderly are often unable to attend social functions or to pursue meaningful social relationships.

—Inability or lack of opportunity to pursue formerly pleasurable activities. Often because of diminished health or lack of mobility, the elderly are cut off from activities that gave their lives pleasure and richness.

—Personal losses through death of friends and family. According to one study, 25 percent of men age 75 and over are widowers; 70 percent of women aged 75 and over are widows.

—Loss of financial resources and worry about financial obligations. The increased incidence of ill health and the need to pay for medical services aggravate stress.

—Isolation. Because of their greater isolation, early symptoms of depression among the elderly are likely to be missed. Often the illness will not be detected until it has advanced to a serious stage.

33. *Can the elderly be treated for depression?*

Not only can they be treated by all the traditional means, but they must. No person deserves to be forsaken to depression.

In an essay on treatment of depression among the elderly, Leo Hollister, M.D., writes:

> The elderly depressed patient requires treatment with no less sense of urgency than the younger patient with depression. One must take a generally conservative approach to treating these patients, as the possibility of an increased number of side effects is very real. If tricyclic antidepressants do not work, one should consider the possible use of monoamine oxidase inhibitors. If suicide is a high risk, electroconvulsive therapy should be considered. Fortunately, most patients will respond to one or another of the pharmacological treatments.
>
> *Depression and Aging* p. 155

34. *What else can be done for the depressed elderly?*

One of the greatest threats to the elderly in general is the sudden amount of free or empty time after busy lives. The loss of occupations and responsibilities often calls into question an individual's sense of self-worth. Help must be given to provide meaningful activities. These may occur in several ways.

1. Community support systems. Many communities provide special activities for the elderly through recreation programs, continuing education programs, library

delivery programs, or social activities. Often the elderly have to be made aware of such programs and provided transportation to them.

2. Family support systems. Visits by family members remain one of the most important support networks. Regular visits for a meal together or shopping trips are essential. It is important to have the elderly visit in the family's home. The family remains the primary community for loving affirmation.

3. Church support systems. In addition to regular visits by pastors, elders, and deacons, churches should supply transportation to worship services or a means for communion services in the elderly person's residence. Many churches have also started tape ministries whereby tapes of services are delivered to the elderly.

35. *One hears increasingly about "post-abortion trauma and depression." How prevalent is it?*

Simply by considering the staggering number of women—and men are affected also—who have undergone abortion, a figure now in the neighborhood of 15-20 million, one begins to get a sense of the dimensions of the concern. Recent studies, provided by Women Exploited By Abortion (WEBA), indicate that depression associated with abortion often does not fully surface until 6-10 years following the abortion. Since abortion has been legal in the United States since 1973, we have here a time bomb of psychological trauma just beginning to explode.

36. *What is post-abortion depression?*

As with other forms of depression, one begins to understand the psychological phenomenon of post-abortion depression by understanding several related factors.

The physiological dangers and potential complications of abortion have now been carefully documented by objective researchers. These dangers range from a high incidence of retained tissue to hemorrhage to sepsis to death. The effects of this disruption of the natural, physiological process are all too often ignored by abortion clinic personnel, or the woman fails to report them to her own gynecologist. Too often minor problems—unstanched bleeding or cramps—escalate by neglect into threatening situations. If we remind ourselves of the hormonal changes occurring in the pregnant woman, discussed in chapter 4, we are also mindful of a biochemical unpheaval involved in abortion.

A second contributing force, in addition to the physiological trauma, is the fact that abortions are almost always procured under conditions of stress. Few women turn to abortion as a first choice: trauma is inflicted upon the body and no one willingly invites it. The choice is most often made in fear or desperation.

37. Do women receive counseling about this at abortion clinics?

The method of counseling provided is generally "values clarification," with emphasis upon the woman's attitudes at the present. An understanding of the method of "values clarification" counseling may be gained from a pamphlet prepared by the executive director of the National Alliance for Optional Parenthood, a pro-abortion agency. This pamphlet appears in abortion clinics around the country. Following the question, "Am I Parent Material?" the pamphlet responds:

> If you decide to have a child, it'll be a decision that will affect you for the rest of your life. Think about it. . . . Taking responsibility for a new life is awesome.
>
> These questions are designed to raise ideas that you may not have thought about. There are no "right" answers and no "grades"—your answers are "right" for you and may help you decide for yourself whether or not you want

to be a parent. Because we all change, your
answers to some of these questions may
change two, five, even ten years from now.

You *do* have a choice. Check out what you
know and give it some thought. Then do what
seems right to you.

The questionable nature of values clarification counseling is evident here. Its focus is upon the immediate
present. While recognizing future changes, the future
and the past are not brought to bear upon present decisions. This methodology leaves little room for serious
contention with guilt, sadness, or depression.

Furthermore, because of the strong religious and social
pressure against abortion itself, the woman coming to
the clinic is not likely to want to spend any more time
there than necessary. In response to my inquiry, a coun-
selor at one abortion clinic responded that less than 2
percent of women having abortions return to the clinic
for their free of charge post-abortion counseling. Because
79 percent of abortion patients are unmarried, we often
have the situation of a single woman, unwilling to return
to the clinic, but with few other support networks available.

38. *What do feminist movements say about this?*

Increasingly, feminists and abortion survivors are arguing that abortion degrades women, that it in fact less-
ens a woman's view of herself. It begins, of course, with
the procedure itself which is in almost all cases a hurried,
impersonal affair. Increasingly, women are adopting the
thought of Janet Smith who argues in "Abortion as a
Feminist Concern," reprinted in *The Zero People* (Ann
Arbor, Mich.: Servant Books, 1983), that "rather than
being a 'right' of women, abortion is a great disservice
to women, one which reflects both a growing lack of
appreciation among women for those powers and
capacities which are distinctly theirs as women and a

growing despair that women are willing and able to be full participants in society and to make the sometimes noble sacrifices demanded of individuals for the good of society." (p. 77) Smith argues, furthermore, that "abortion is a denial of one of those powers which make women women. Childbearing is basic to them. We might expect that deliberate and violent denial of such a potential may be devastating." (p. 84)

39. That provides some of the reasons for post-abortion depression, but what exactly is it? Does it differ from any other depression?

Many studies have now pointed out the "mental and psychological sequelae"—those psychological effects following an abortion. From his own records, for example, Matthew Buffin, M.D., observed that "from January 1972 to June 1979, I saw 802 patients who had undergone legal abortions. Of these 802 women, 159 (19.9 percent) suffered mental or physical complications of such magnitude or duration as to be considered significantly disabling. Even though 643 patients (80.1 percent) had essentially negative findings upon examination and review of medical history, my impression is that the great majority of these women viewed their experience as painful, traumatic, and one that they would like to forget." (p. 98) Similarly, in hearings before the Senate Subcommittee on the Constitution of the Committee of the Judiciary, Vincent Rue, a professor of family relations at California State University, Los Angeles, argued that

> Abortion is a psychological Trojan Horse for women. Countless authors have exclaimed the merits of this medical procedure and asserted only temporary, nonpathological, and limited adverse emotional sequelae. Yet the only consistent, positive reaction reported in an exhaustive literature review is that of relief. . . . Negative feelings may include guilt,

> anxiety, depression, a sense of loss, anger,
> relational changes with partner, a feeling of
> being misled by misinformation or lack of in-
> formation, deterioration of self- image, regret
> or remorse, nightmares. . . (from Hearings
> Records, 97th Congress).

Several years ago, the Stritch School of Medicine of Loyola University held a conference devoted to the psychological aspects of abortion. The essays were subsequently collected in a book, *The Psychological Aspects of Abortion* (Washington, D.C.: University Publications of America, 1979). One of the studies, directed by Monte Harris Liebman, M.D., surveyed recent research of the psychological effects of abortion, finding common sequelae of "guilt, shame, fear, loss, anger, resentment, depression, or remorse" (p. 127).

Examples such as these are representative of a wide sample of surveys, clinical studies, and observations from private medical records. Perhaps the most thorough report to date is provided in *Rachel Weeping* (San Francisco: Harper & Row, 1984), by James T. Burtchaell. Such examples do indicate the severe emotional impact of abortion. The significant reminder is that many of these reactions are delayed, sometimes not surfacing until 6-10 years after the abortion.

40. *Are only women affected?*

The effects are not relegated to women alone. Nearly forgotten in the entire abortion controversy is the man who fathered the child and retains no rights to that child under current law. Since many of the psychological consequences of abortion upon women have to do with the loss of the unborn child, it is not unreasonable to point out that many men participate in the sense of loss and suffer many of the same psychological manifestations.

41. *What can be done to meet this need?*

To be sure, the post-abortion depressive may need professional, medical help as does any depressed person, but the Christian community has a unique opportunity to act in the Christlike fashion of forgiveness and servanthood here, for only Christian forgiveness, love, and acceptance can supply the final answers for the overwhelming questions of the post-abortion depressive. John Powell, S.J., Professor of Theology at Loyola University, strikes the proper spirit when he pleads:

> Let's be sure to speak out of love, however, not out of judgment or hatred toward those who perform or who have had abortions. I have been involved with a lot of prolife work, and I'm convinced that one thing that could short circuit this whole movement would be for it to become infected with vindictiveness or hate. If we want to stand up for the sacredness of human life, we have to speak up out of love—love for the babies who won't see life, and for the frightened women who often don't understand what they're going through, and even for abortionists who somehow believe that the killing is necessary. We can judge the action of abortion and say loudly and clearly that it is terribly wrong, but we should not take on ourselves God's role in judging the subjective responsibility of individuals.
>
> (*The Zero People*, p. 10)

One organization modeled upon this view is Women Exploited By Abortion (WEBA), which now has chapters in every state. WEBA was formed for women who have endured an abortion, who recognize the evil of the act, and who seek healing in God's name.

The healing process, WEBA believes, must begin by recognizing grief and guilt and allowing it to surface. The woman who has aborted, WEBA believes, needs acceptance, but she also needs forgiveness to allay the guilt and begin life anew. WEBA recognizes that the miracle of healing comes ultimately from Jesus. WEBA believes that "Joy comes in the Mourning"—its adopted slogan—only because Jesus has promised to wipe away every tear from their cheek.

41. *Could you provide a list of resources for future study on depression?*

1. For general information, you may write to the following:
   Public Inquiries Section
   National Institute of Mental Health
   Room 150-05
   5600 Fishers Lane
   Rockville, MD 20857

   Canadian Mental Health Association
   National Office
   2160 Yonge St.
   Toronto, Ontario M4S 2Z3

2. General resources in most public libraries are the following:
   Diagnostic and Statistical Manual of Mental Resources. 3d ed. Washington, D.C.: American Psychiatric Association, 1980.
   Berkow, Robert, ed. *The Merck Manual*. 14th ed. Rahway, NJ: Merck, 1987.

3. For commonly prescribed drugs and their side effects consult *The Physician's Desk Reference*, available in most public libraries.

4. Books and articles referred to in this study and related books written for a lay audience include the following:

Baker, Don and Nester, Emery. *Depression: Finding Hope and Meaning in Life's Darkest Shadow.* Portland, Ore.: Multnomah Press, 1983.

Barrett, Roger. *Depression: What It Is and What to Do about It*. Elgin, Ill.: David C. Cook, 1977.

Beck, Aaron T. *Depression: Causes and Treatment*. Philadelphia: University of Pennsylvania Press, 1967.

Berg, Richard F., and McCartney, Christine. *Depression and the Integrated Life: A Christian Understanding of Sadness and Inner Suffering*. New York: Alba House, 1981.

Breslau, Lawrence D., and Haug, Marie R., eds. *Depression and Aging*. New York: Springer Publishers, 1983.

Brodsky, Annette M., and Mustin, Rachel T. Hare, eds. *Women and Psychotherapy: An Assessment of Research and Practice*. New York: The Guilford Press, 1980.

Burns, Lawrence S., ed. "The World of the Brain." *Harper's Magazine*. December, 1975.

Burtchaell, James T. *Rachel Weeping*. San Francisco: Harper & Row, 1984.

Dix, Carol. *The New Mother Syndrome: Coping with Postpartum Stress and Depression*. Garden City: Doubleday, 1985.

Eble, Diane. "Too Young to Die." *Christianity Today*, March 20, 1987, pp. 19-24.

Frazer, Alan and Winokur, Andrew. *Biological Bases of Psychiatric Disorders*. New York: Spectrum Publications, 1977.

Gallagher, Winifred. "The Dark Affliction of Mind and Body," *Discover*. May, 1986, pp. 66-76.

Grissen, Lillian V. "His Way Is in the Sea." *The Banner*, 14 October 1985, pp. 7-9.

Grissen, Ray. "Coping with Depression." *The Banner*, 14 October 1985, pp. 10-11.

Hensley, Jeff, ed. *The Zero People*. Ann Arbor, Mich.: Servant Books, 1983.

"Hormones" *Newsweek*. 12 January 1987, pp. 50-59.

Jansma, Theodore. *Toward a Christian Psychotherapy*. Cherry Hill, NJ: Mack Publishing Company, 1973.

Keen, Ernest. "Emerging from Depression," *American Behavioral Scientist* 27 (July/August 1984): 801-12.

Plantinga, Cornelius, Jr. "A Love So Fierce," *The Reformed Journal* (November 1986).

Saks, Bonnie R. "Depressed Mood During Pregnancy and the Puerperium," *American Journal of Psychiatry* 142 (June 1985): 728-31.

Sheehan, David V. *The Anxiety Disease*. New York: Charles Scribners, 1983.

Smedes, Lewis B. *Forgive and Forget*. New York: Harper & Row, 1984.

Tsuang, Ming T., and Vandermey, Randall. *Genes and the Mind*. New York: Oxford University Press, 1980.

Vander Goot, Mary. "Depressed or Just Discouraged?" *The Banner*, 14 October 1985, pp. 12-13.

Wangerin, Walter, Jr. *The Orphean Passages*. San Francisco: Harper & Row, 1986.

Wetzel, Janice Wood. *Clinical Handbook of Depression*. New York: Gardiner Books, 1984.

White, John. *The Masks of Melancholy*. Downers Grove, Ill.: InterVarsity Press, 1982.

Youngs, Bettie B. *Stress in Children: How to Recognize, Avoid and Overcome It*. New York: Arbor House, 1985.

Notes

1. Emily Dickinson, "There Came a Day," *The Poems of Emily Dickinson*, Thomas H. Johnson, ed. (Cambridge: Harvard University Press, 1955).

2. Philip Yancey, *Open Windows* (Nashville: Thomas Nelson, 1985), p. 162.

3. Emily Dickinson, "Pain Has an Element of Blank," *The Poems of Emily Dickinson*, Thomas H. Johnson, ed. (Cambridge: Harvard University Press, 1955).

4. *Diagnostic and Statistical Manual of Mental Disorders*, 3d ed. (Washington, D.C.: American Psychiatric Association, 1980.

5. Mary Vander Goot, "Depressed or Just Discouraged?" *The Banner*, October 14, 1985, p. 13.

6. Ibid.

7. Winifred Gallagher, "The Dark Affliction of Mind and Body," *Discover* (May, 1986), p. 67.

8. Walter Wangerin, Jr., *The Orphean Passages* (San Francisco: Harper & Row, 1986), p. 11.

9. Lawrence S. Burns, "The World of the Brain," *Harper's Magazine* (December, 1975), p. 7.

10. Roger Barrett, *Depression: What It Is and What to Do about It* (Elgin, Ill.: David C. Cook, 1977), p. 198.

11. Ibid., p. 199.

12. Lillian V. Grissen, "His Way Is in the Sea," *The Banner* (October 14, 1985), pp. 7-9.

13. Ibid.

14. Annette M. Brodsky and Rachel T. Hare-Mustin, eds., *Women and Psychotherapy: An Assessment of Research and Practice* (New York: The Guilford Press, 1980), p. 331.

15. Ibid.

16. Alan Frazer and Andrew Winokur, *Biological Bases of Psychiatric Disorders* (New York: Spectrum Publications, 1977), pp. 220-21.

17. Carol Dix, *The New Mother Syndrome: Coping with Postpartum Stress and Depression* (Garden City: Doubleday, 1985), p. XIV.

18. Ibid, pp. 19-20.

19. Ibid. p. 19.

20. Ibid., p. 23.

21. *Newsweek*, January 12, 1987, p. 52.

22. Ibid.

23. *American Journal of Psychiatry*, (July 1985), p. 730.

24. Ibid.

25. Ibid., p. 728.

26. Ibid., p. 730.

27. Cornelius Plantinga, Jr., "A Love So Fierce," *The Reformed Journal*, (November 1986).

28. Ibid.

29. Grissen, Ray, "Coping with Depression," *The Banner*, (October 14, 1985).

30. G. A. Young, "God Leads Us Along."

31. John White, *The Masks of Melancholy* (Downers Grove, Ill.: InterVarsity Press, 1982), p. 213.

32. Ibid., P. 214.

33. Janet Wood Wetzel, *Clinical Handbook of Depression* (New York: Gardiner Books, 1984), p. 257.

34. Ibid., p. 258.

35. Ibid., p. 216.

36. Ernest Keen, "Emerging from Depression," *American Behavioral Scientist* (July/August 1984), p. 804.

37. Ibid., p. 808.

38. Tim Stafford, *Knowing the Face of God* (Grand Rapids: Zondervan, 1986), p. 226.